Can Any Guitarist Even Dream? Vol1 Beginnings

Table of Contents

Author: Steven M. Ono, 2019 Cover Photo: Karena Beasley, 2009 Editors: Karena Beasley and Pat Wolk ISBN 9780692193525

Guitar Parts

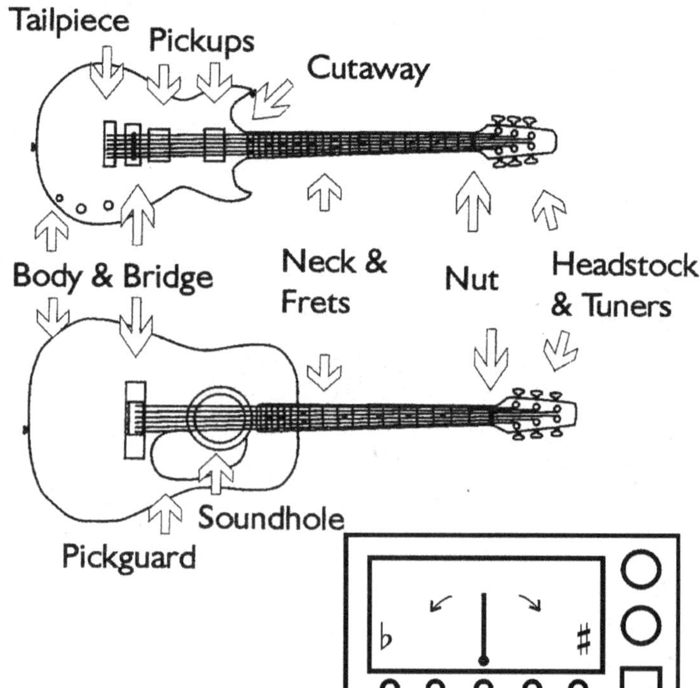

Head stock, Neck & Body

The strings are numbered 1 through 6, from thin to thick. We turn the tuning knobs on the head stock up or down in order to tune up each string. The neck has the fingerboard and frets which are numbered from the nut to the sound hole.

When holding the guitar, higher is better. While most players rest the guitar on their laps, mostly the right hip using the right elbow and body to hold the instrument, using a guitar strap will help stabilize the guitar even if you are sitting down.

Tuning is absolutely the most important thing you will do with your guitar. I would rather have people play air guitar than out of tune guitar because air guitar sounds good.

Out of tune sounds BAD. In tune sounds GOOD.
E6 A5 D4 G3 B2 E1 from low to high strings.

Eddie Ate Dynamite Good Bye Eddie

Too low is flat and too high is sharp.

Electronic tuners. Some guitar tuners only recognize the notes of the open strings of the guitar/bass. A chromatic tuner can tune to any note so make sure it is the right note. **Crutch or tool?** If you tune the low E to your electronic tuner then tune the rest of the strings by ear you can use the electronic tuner to check your ear's accuracy.

Tuning By Ear The 5th & 4th Frets

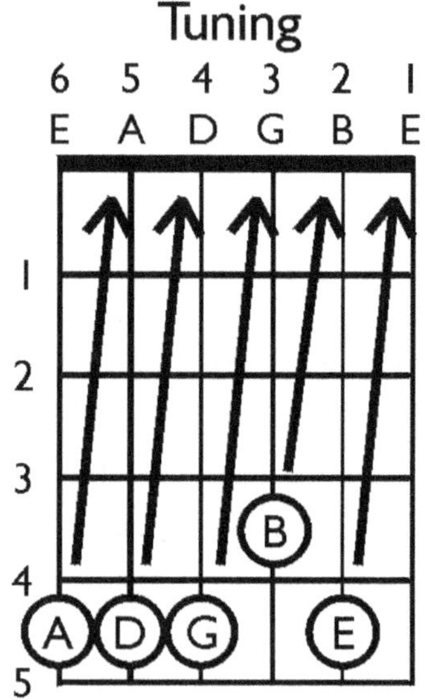

Turn the tuning knob counter-clockwise for higher pitch and clockwise for lower pitch. In standard tuning all strings are tuned at the 5th fret except the 2nd string which is tuned from the 3rd string 4th fret B.

The Wobble or Wave Tune the low E string to a tuner or a piano. Press the 6th string down at the 5th fret. Pick the 6th and open 5th strings and let them ring together. Listen for wobble.

The 1st question: Is it out of tune? If the two strings wave at all, the answer is yes! If it is a slow wave you are very close!

The 2nd question: Is it too high or too low? Sharp or flat? Sing with each strings' note and listen to the pitch change of your own voice. As the two pitches get closer the wobble becomes slower like a wave. When the wave slows to a stop the string is in tune. Farther apart the wobble becomes faster.

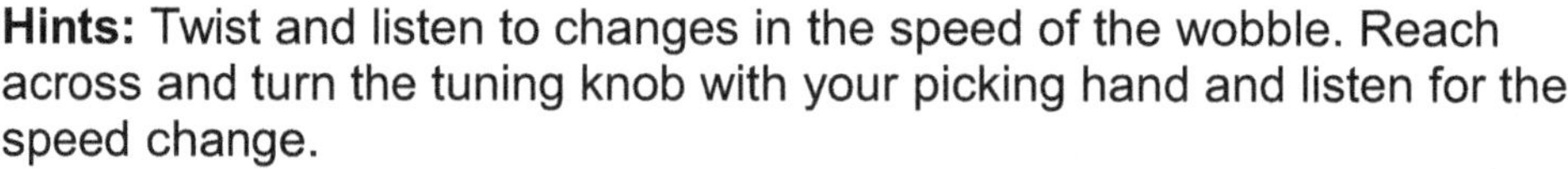

Hints: Twist and listen to changes in the speed of the wobble. Reach across and turn the tuning knob with your picking hand and listen for the speed change.

Do not turn the tuner unless you can hear both strings. Remember: slower is closer, faster is farther away. When the wave stops you are in tune!

Picking

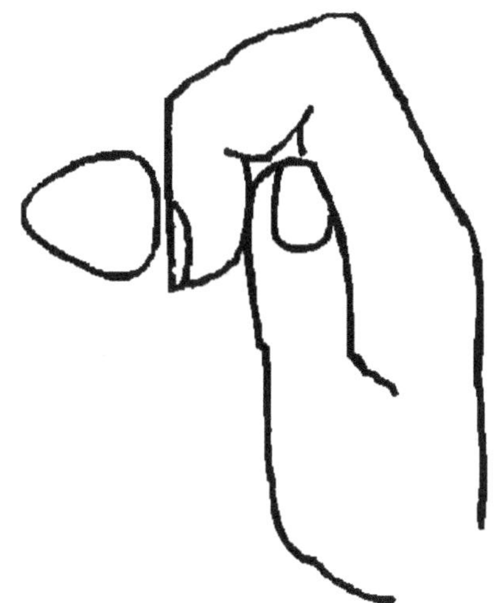

Holding the pick between the thumb & side of forefinger. Touch as much of the surface of the pick as you can. Squeeze the pick gently letting it bounce a bit under your thumb. Keep the pick pointed straight at the top of the guitar. Strike the string(s) gently.

Picking is plucking individual notes on individual strings one at a time. Move the pick only enough to strike the string, Pick each string down/up.
Strumming is striking two or more strings at once. Strum two strings down / up then three strings, four strings, five strings and finally, all six strings.

Finger picking

The right hand fingers can be used to pluck the guitar's strings instead of the pick.
Generally the three lower strings are thumb territory and the higher strings are finger territory.
Relax your wrist as much as possible.
Pick a low string with the side of your thumb then pick across each of the three higher strings with each of the fingers.
Pinch them all together and in thumb and single finger pairs.

Strum Direction
Down V Up Λ

PIMA is the acronym for the Spanish words for the right hand fingers:
Pulgar, Indice, Medio y Anular or Thumb Index Middle Ring.

Right Hand Fingers:	Thumb	Index	Middle	Ring
Folk Fingerstyle:	T	I	M	R
Classical Guitar:	P	I	M	A

Besides playing chord arpeggios, the fingers can play scale lines by using alternating fingers: i m i m is the favorite but we also use m i m i, m a m a, a m a m, ami, ima. Any possible combination can be used.

Free Strokes: Pluck the string with a fingertip and stay in the air. Do not touch the next string.

Rest Strokes: Play the first string with the i m i m technique. rest the fingertip on the second string after plucking the first.

Pulgar strikes the string with the side of the finger, not the tip, in a circular motion.

Keep the thumb in front of the fingers not behind.

Fingering

Touch the string as close to the fret as possible with the fingertip only. Keep your knuckles arched, fingers spread apart and your thumb at the back of the neck, not hooked over the top!

Squeeze the string to the neck as lightly as you can and still get the sound. Do not flop the fingertips!

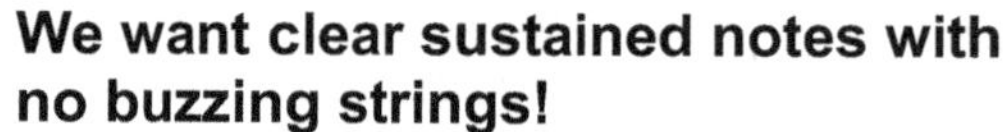

We want clear sustained notes with no buzzing strings!

4 Fingers 4 Frets

This is the basic philosophy of good lead guitar and a great exercise for the left hand. Start with the thumb arched back and placed at the center of the neck with the fingers curled and pointed at the fingerboard. Spreading the fingers apart, strengthening and supporting the 4th finger are critical. Lean the hand into the curled up 4th & 3rd fingers. The 1st finger has a capability to stretch back.

Go For a Walk

Each pair of fingers must be exercised. **Caution!** Start this exercise at the 7th fret if your hand is too small to play any lower on the neck. Every finger pair should walk all over the neck learning to stretch the fingers farther apart as they go lower.

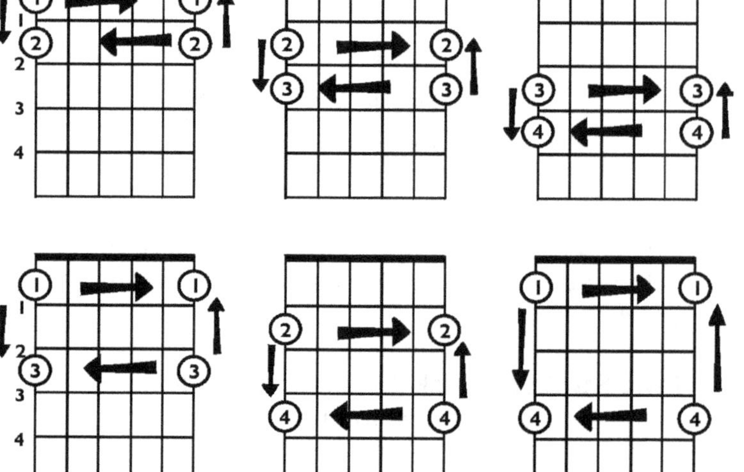

Going up!

1. Pick the 6th string with the 1st finger on a starting fret,
2. place the 2nd finger in front of the 1st at the next fret and pick it while lifting off the 1st finger to
3. walk to the the 5th string, pick that note,
4. place the 2nd finger in front of the 1st at the next fret, pick it while lifting off the 1st finger.

Going down!

1. Place the 2nd finger at a starting fret on the 1st string and pick that note while placing the 1st finger behind the 2nd at the next lowest fret.
2. Lift the 2nd finger and pick the 1st finger's note.
3. Place the 2nd finger at the starting fret 2nd string and pick that note while placing the 1st finger behind the 2nd at the next lowest fret.
4. Lift the 2nd finger and pick the 1st finger's note.

When you walk one foot is always on the ground while the other is lifting off. Each pair of fingers must be exercised in the same way. **Pick each string cleanly, slowly & deliberately.**

4/4 Time and Beat Counting

The common time signature is **C** or 4/4 meaning four quarter notes per measure or bar. The top number indicates how many notes. The bottom number tells us what kind of note gets the beat count.

4/4 AKA
Common Time
4 Beats
Quarter Note

Count to four over and over.

If the tempo (speed) is slow enough you should be able to make any chord change on time for the next beat.

Note & Rest Values

Note & Rest Values show note timing and duration. Notes are sounds while rests are silences. A whole note and whole rest are counted with four beats. Half note, quarter notes and eighth notes in 4/4 time work together exactly like fractions of an inch.

Draw the treble clef. Make a vertical line extending above and below the staff. Then draw "the squiggle". Draw bar lines and draw note heads, both hollow and solid. Stems go up on the right if the note head is below the middle line and down on the left if the note head is above. Stems are a vertical line one octave long. Draw slash notes which indicate chord strums. Draw repeat signs which indicate a repeating section of music.

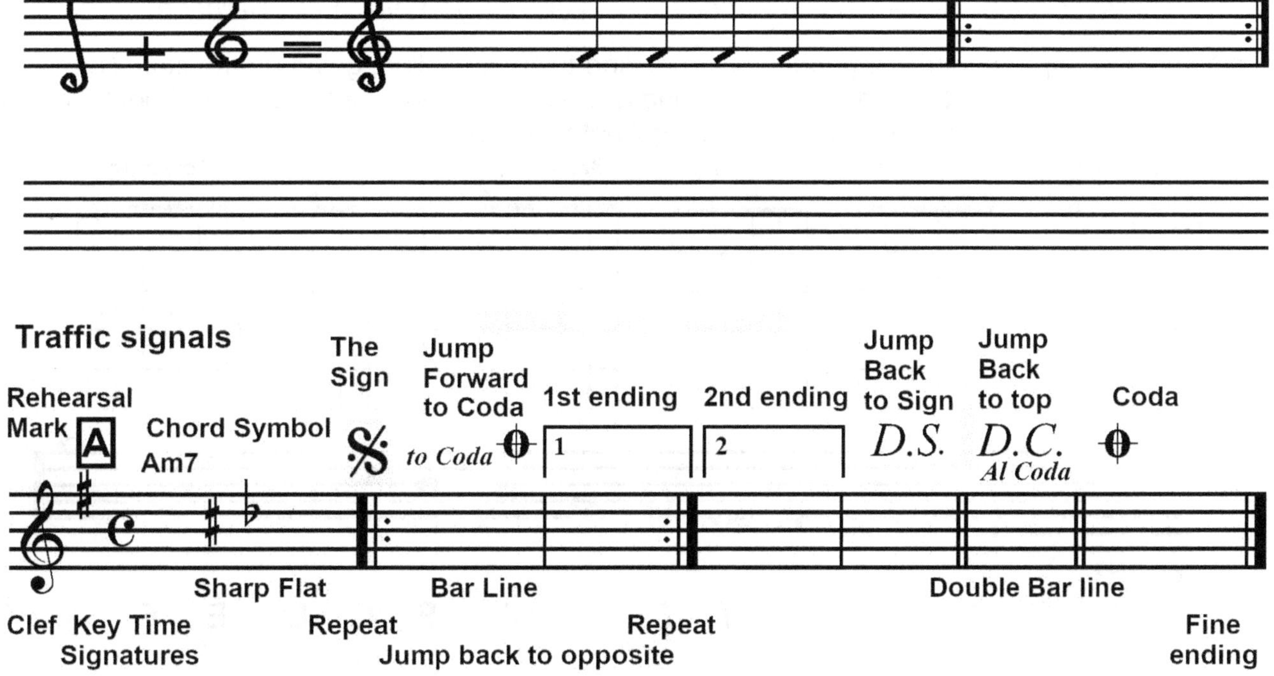

The Neck Map and the Musical Alphabet

The musical alphabet is ABCDEFG going up and GFEDCBA going down in whole steps and half steps, two frets and one fret.
White dots are white keys. Every natural note is a whole step apart except E & F and B & C. These are the only two natural half steps.

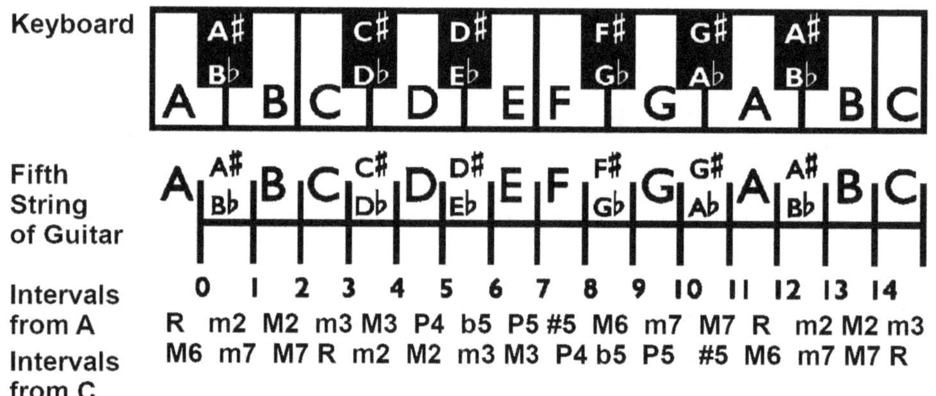

Fret	6	5	4	3	2	1
	E	A	D	G	B	E
1	F	A# Bb	D# Eb	G# Ab	C	F
2	F# Gb	B	E	A	C# Db	F# Gb
3	G	C	F	A# Bb	D	G
4	G# Ab	C# Db	F# Gb	B	D# Eb	G# Ab
5	A	D	G	C	E	A
6	A# Bb	D# Eb	G# Ab	C# Db	F	A# Bb
7	B	E	A	D	F# Gb	B
8	C	F	A# Bb	D# Eb	G	C
9	C# Db	F# Gb	B	E	G# Ab	C# Db
10	D	G	C	F	A	D
11	D# Eb	G# Ab	C# Db	F# Gb	A# Bb	D# Eb
12	E	A	D	G	B	E

The black dots between every other pair of notes are the sharps and flats. Think of the neck of the guitar as six long main streets (strings) and twelve cross streets (frets). At each intersection (address) a note lives!

The Treble Clef and Staff

Lines and Spaces There are a couple of mnemonic devices used to help memorize the lines and spaces of the treble clef and staff: Every Good Boy Does Fine and FACE. But I prefer the funnier sayings:

Elvis' Guitar Broke Down Friday and Fat Alley Cats Eat Garbage.

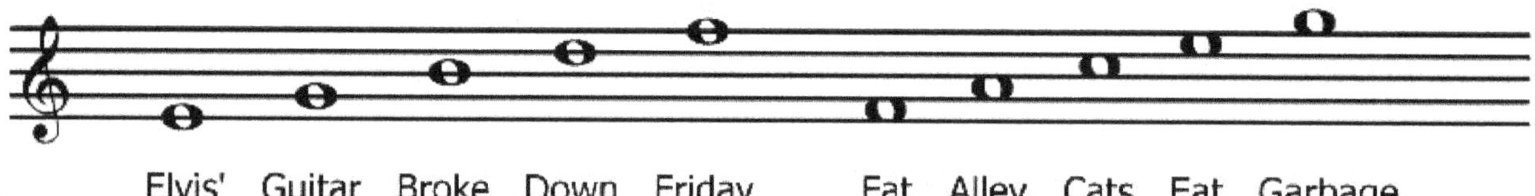

Elvis' Guitar Broke Down Friday Fat Alley Cats Eat Garbage

The note names are arranged in alphabetical order, line to space to line, going up the staff. Note heads get placed either "in the space", not crossing a line on either side or "on the line", not touching the lines on either side. The lowest two bass strings' notes are on ledger lines.

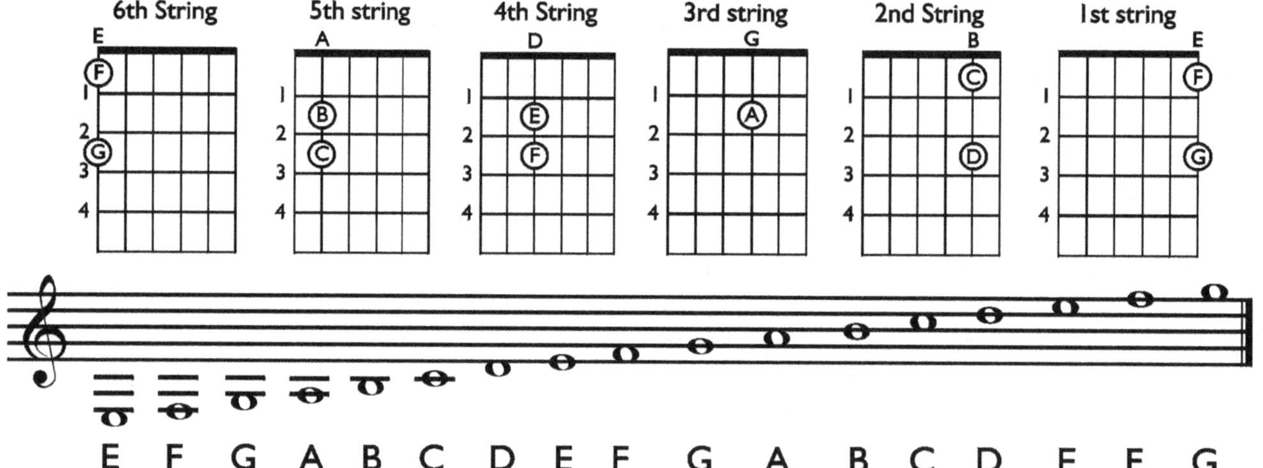

Chords C and G7 **Basic finger hopping**

Start fingering these chords with the 3rd finger first then the 2nd and 1st fingers. The 3rd finger holds the bass note of the chord and gets the highest priority.
More about bass notes next.

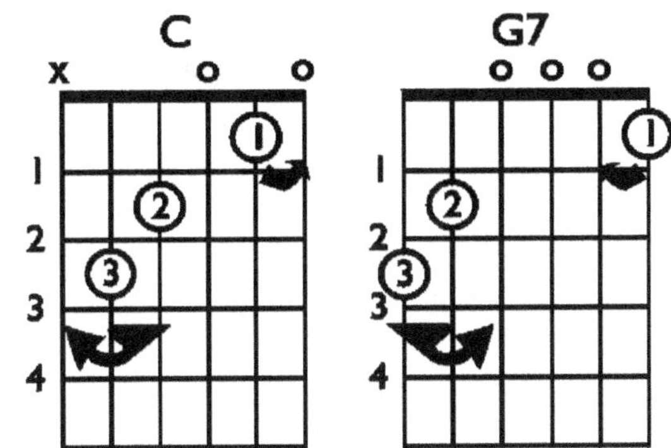

1. Lift the 1st finger.
2. Finger hop the 3rd and 2nd fingers to 6th & 5th strings.
3. Place the 1st finger at the 1st string 1st fret by stretching it back to the note. The fingers are spread out over 3 frets. Try splitting the chord into upper and lower movements.

The chord symbol **C** is for the **C major chord**. **G7** is for the **G dominant seventh chord.**

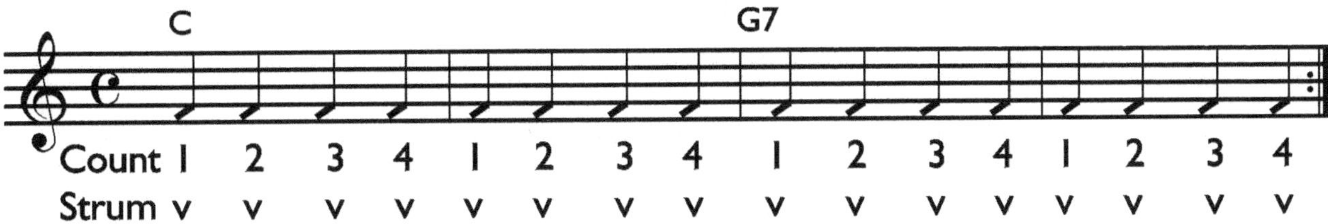

These note heads, called rhythm slashes, are used to indicate a chord strum. The repeat sign is the double dots, thin line and thick line at the end of the staff.

A to E

A

E

1. Lift the 1st finger.
2. Hop the 2nd & 3rd fingers together to 5th & 4th strings.
3. Place the 1st finger on 3rd string at the 1st fret. Move in reverse to get back.

Make the changes, stay on the beat

Tap your foot and count to four over and over very slowly. Strum the first chord four times twice and change carefully to the next chord. Strum the guitar with your wrist, not your elbow. Strum the next chord four times twice and change back. Keep the count very slow so you have more time to change chords quickly after the second beat 4 and before beat 1 comes back around.
The chord symbol A is for the A major chord.

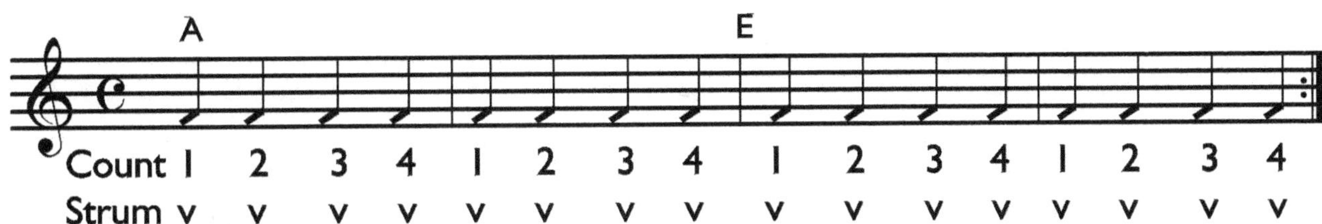

Repeat these exercises 50 to 100 times per day and the chord changes will become easier.

NOTES: The 1st and 2nd String

The 1st String open is the E as in Eat, the 1st string 1st fret is the F as in Friday and the 1st string 3rd fret is the G as in Garbage.

The 2nd String open is the B as in Broke, the 2nd string 1st fret is the C as in Cats and the 2nd string 3rd fret is the D as in Down.

Finger seating: Keep the 1st finger at the first fret while pressing the 3rd finger at third fret.

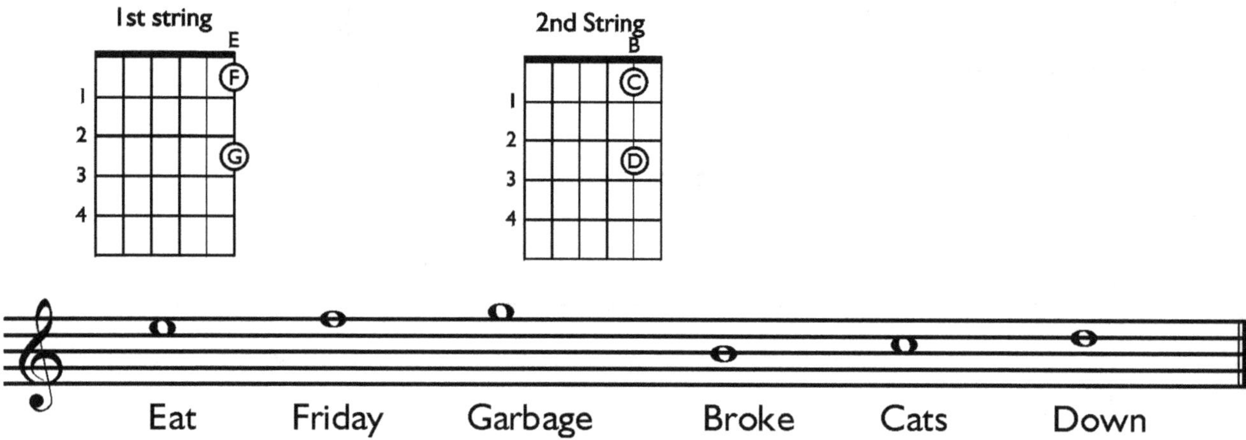

Lazy Guitarist Credo: "If I don't need to lift a finger... I won't."

Mystery Tunes!

Here's a part of a tune. Can you figure out the rest of it?

This is beginning of the Ode to Joy by Beethoven. How does the rest of the tune go?
Figure it out and write it down. Modern charts often don't include a clef at the beginning of each line.

Flats, Sharps & Naturals:

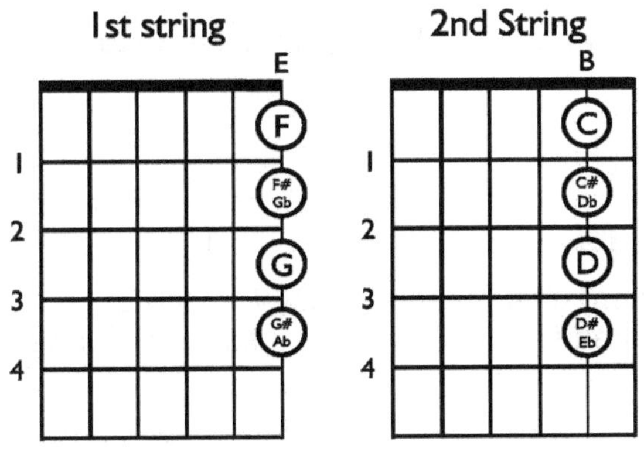

The note map in the front of this book has white circles for the natural notes and black circles for the accidentals: flats & sharps.

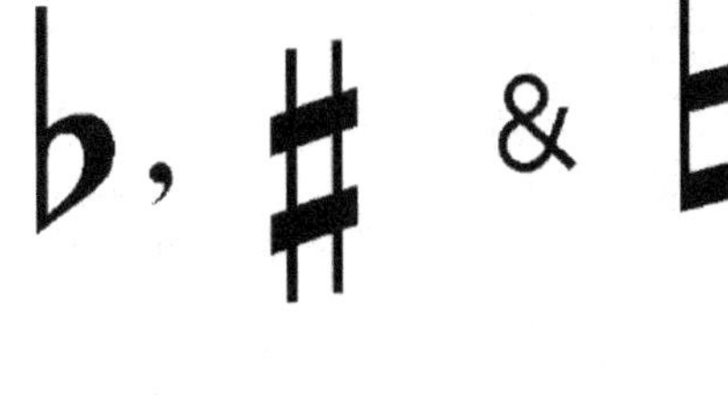

A flat makes the note a half step lower than normal pitch and a sharp makes the note one half step higher than the normal. A natural is a sharp or flat fixer!

Every other key than C/Am uses flats or sharps.

The key of G/Em uses F# or the raised 7th and the key of F/Dm uses Bb or a lower 4th. They are indicated by a key signature.

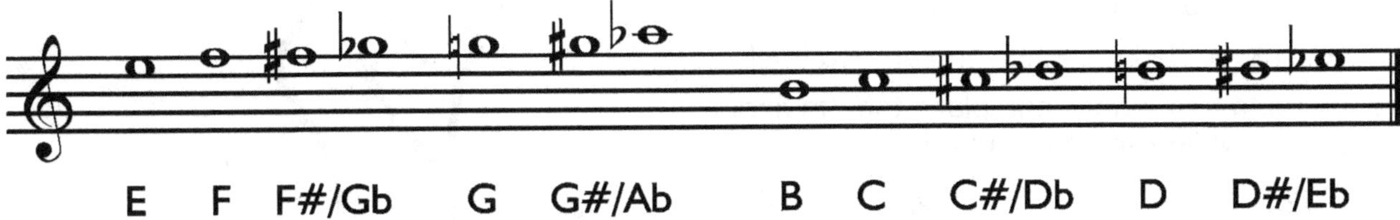

They can also be added on a note by note basis. The 1st string has an F#/Gb at the 2nd fret and G#/Ab at the 4th. The 2nd string has a C#/Db at the 2nd fret and a D#/Eb at the 4th.

It is important to remember that you can sharp an open string but you cannot flat one.

Major & Minor

Good Guys & Bad Guys One – Six I - VIm In the theater, movies and TV, the musical score will usually reflect the kind of character being presented. Major keys & chords would be played for the good guys and minor keys & chords for the bad guys.

C Am

Shared Finger

In a major key the relative minor is the sixth chord counted from the major I chord. Count on your fingers from one to six, no zeros. C D E F G A B C

1 2 3 4 5 6 7 8

The Bad Guy's number is 6.

In a minor key the relative major is the III (3) chord counted from the minor I (1) Chord. Count on your fingers from one to three, no zeros. A B C D E F G A

1 2 3 4 5 6 7 8

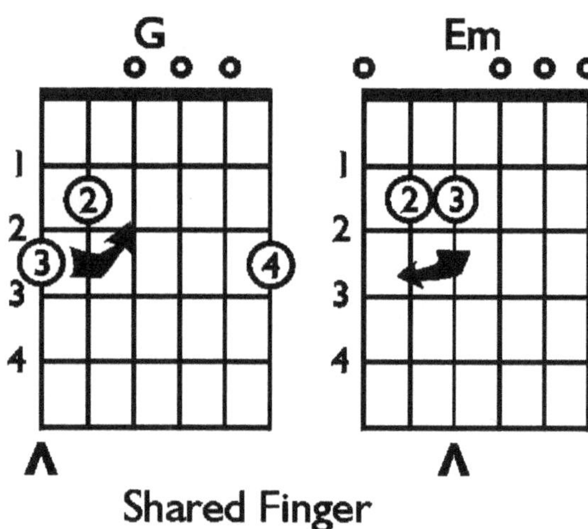

Shared Finger

The Good Guy's number is 3.

It is all about the center of gravity. C or Am: which is number 1?

What's the relative minor of G major?

Write the letters of the musical alphabet from G to the next highest G.

Shared Fingers

Both the C - Am chord change and the G - Em chord change involve shared fingers with the 3rd finger from one side of the 2nd finger to the other.

The Pinky Trick

This G major fingering uses the 4th finger (the pinky!) and is more versatile than most other fingerings.

1) Keep the pinky curled up tightly and arched back.

2) Move the hand to the neck and place the 4th finger on the 1st string while keeping it curled.

Arch the fingers back at the hand and operate them like little hammers, always landing on the tips. Think of a claw with talons spread.

We use all four fingers of the left hand to play guitar!

Notes on The 3rd & 4th Strings

The 3rd string has two natural notes: G & A or guitar alley.

The 4th string is your highest bass string and has three natural notes: D, E & F. The 4th string has bass notes of chords. This could be spelled out using: dead elvis fat.

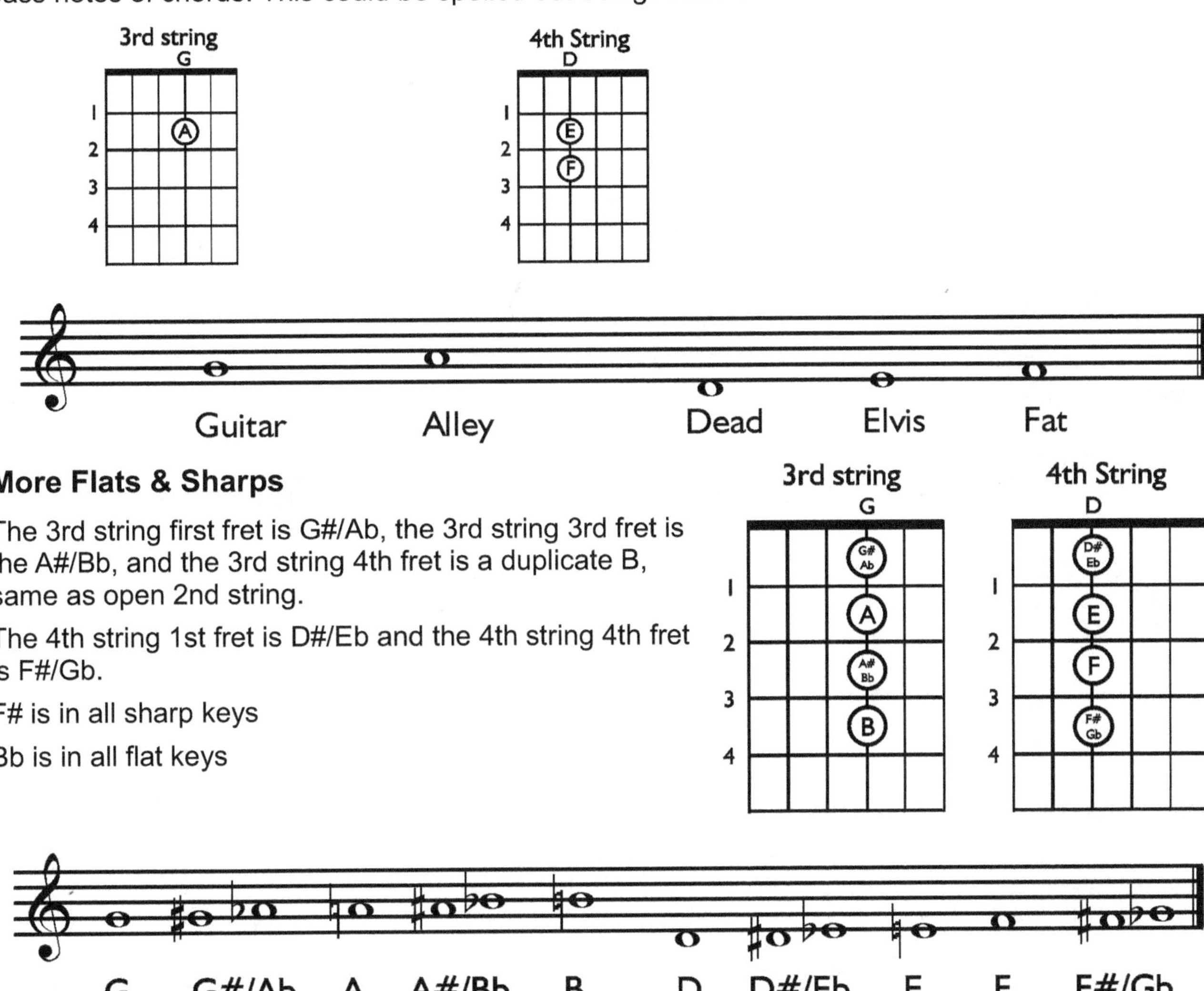

More Flats & Sharps

The 3rd string first fret is G#/Ab, the 3rd string 3rd fret is the A#/Bb, and the 3rd string 4th fret is a duplicate B, same as open 2nd string.

The 4th string 1st fret is D#/Eb and the 4th string 4th fret is F#/Gb.

F# is in all sharp keys

Bb is in all flat keys

Draw these new sharp and flat notes and higher on the upcoming blank staves along with the natural notes you already know, using the natural sign. Do it as randomly as you can. After you have drawn them write the name of the note under each note head, plot them in a chord block and play them on your guitar.

Two Kinds of A chords: Major and Minor

A and Am are triad chords which share notes with each other, including the bass note A (open 5th string) but they are NOT in the same Key. The difference is the C natural note in the Am chord and the C# note in the A chord. These notes are the minor 3rd and major 3rd of A: A1 B2 C3.

The 3rd note counted from A has to be C something.

In this case the minor 3rd is C (1st fret 2nd string) and the major 3rd is C# (2nd fret 2nd string).

The only time you will see the number 3 in any chord name is if it says "no3rd."

Ano3rd means neither 3rd C natural or C# are welcome in the chord only the root A and the 5th E or the lowest three strings of either A or Am. This chord is also known as **A5** and is also called an **open power chord**.

3/4 Time: The Waltz

4/4 or common time has four quarter notes per bar, A waltz or 3/4 has three quarter notes.

Count	1	2	3	1	2	3	1	2	3	1	2	3
Strum	v	v	v	v	v	v	v	v	v	v	v	v

Music Theory

The Key of C Major is made of the C major scale and its triad chords. It is the only key with no flats or sharps. Traditionally, scale steps are numbered with Arabic numerals 1 - 7 and chords are numbered with Roman numerals I - VII. The C major scale is all of the plain alphabet notes or white circles on the neck map.

C	D	E	F	G	A	B	C
1	2	3	4	5	6	7	8

Count the scale! C1 D2 E3 F4 G5 A6 B7 C8 Pick each of these notes alphabetically from the bass note C up to the higher C and you will hear the familiar do re mi major scale. Play it backwards too.

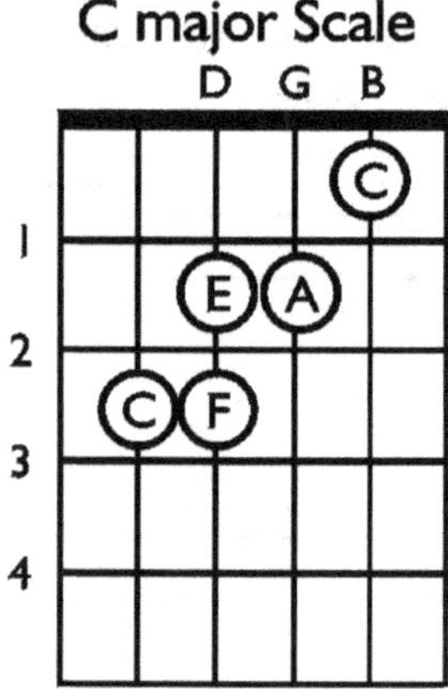

Notes are like individual alphabet letters and chords are like words, groups of letters, in the language of music.

The C triad chord is built from every other note in the scale from the root note: root, 3rd and 5th: C, E and G.

Each chord and note relationship has a distinct sound.

Each sound reveals a chord and note relationship if you learn to recognize them.

Chord/Note Relationship/Harmonic Analysis

Mary Had a Little Lamb steps down from E to D to C and back up to E. E is the third of the C chord so that movement works out to 3212333 in scale steps in relation to the C chord. When it gets to the DDD

the note D is no longer the the 2 of C but it is now the 5 of the G7 chord: GABCD.

The tune above starts on the root or 1, jumps to the 3 and then 5 of the C chord. What are the relationships of the notes in the second measure to the G7 chord? Figure it out for the whole tune. Harmonic analysis is a great tool.

Pick out this tune by ear. From any note in a melody the next note can do one of three things:

1) It can repeat
2) It can go higher on the musical alphabet
3) It can go lower on the musical alphabet

Figure out the rest and write it down.

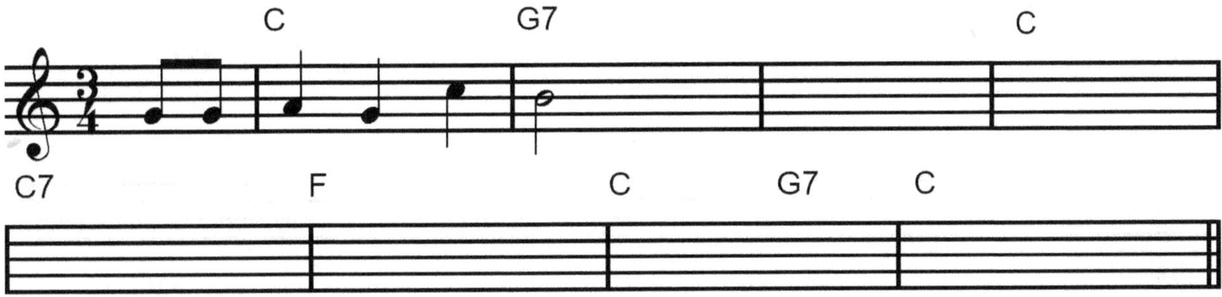

Melodic Motion

Neighbor Notes

The name is pretty obvious. Both above and below each chord tone the nearest note is a neighbor note. Go for a visit and come back.

Against a C chord CDC is 121, EFE is 343 and GAG is 565, These are upper neighbor notes.

CBC is 171, EDE is 323 and GFG is 545 are lower neighbor notes.

Passing Tones

Between the chord tones are passing tones. Each non chord tone can be used like a stepping stone to the next chord tone up or down. Ascending: CDE is 123, EFG is 345, GBC is 571 and GAC is 561.

Suspensions

Playing a non chord tone on a strong beat then moving to a chord tone creates a suspension. The DC is 21, FE is 43, AG is a 65 are descending suspensions. Ascending: BC is 71, DE is 23, FG is 45.

Melodic Leaps go either up or down and are measured by how far the leap is. That distance is called the interval.

Guide Fingers

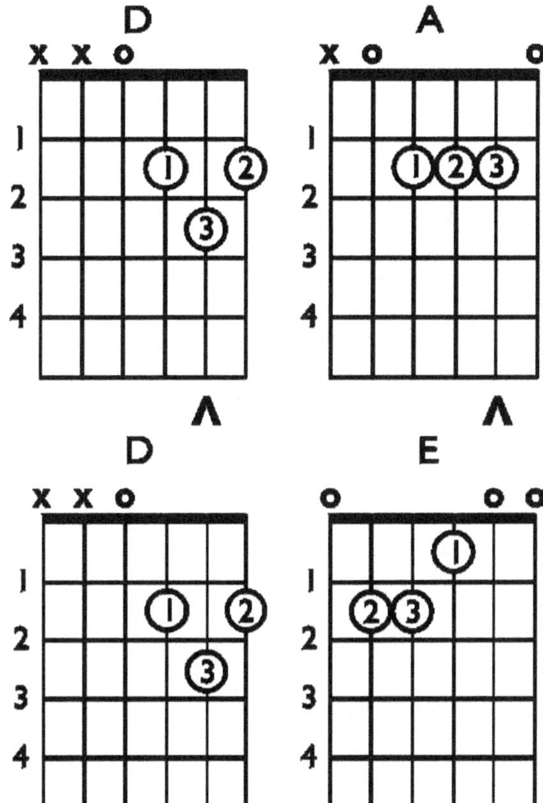

Some chord pairs have a finger that shares the same string at a different fret. This is a guide finger which slides to the next fret. This also introduces the D chord.

A to D

1. Lift 1st & 2nd fingers.
2. Slide the 3rd finger up one fret on the 2nd string.
3. Place 1st & 2nd behind the 3rd finger but split apart on the 3rd and 1st strings.

D to A

1. Lift 1st & 2nd fingers.
2. Slide the 3rd finger back to the 2nd fret.
3. Place 1st & 2nd on the 4th and 3rd strings.

E to D

1. Lift 2nd & 3rd fingers.
2. Slide the 1st finger up one fret.
3. Place 2nd & 3rd fingers into the corner and on the point of the D triangle.

D to E

1. Lift 2nd & 3rd fingers.
2. Slide the 1st finger to the first fret.
3. Place 2nd & 3rd fingers on the 5th and 4th strings behind the 2nd fret.

Any finger can be used as a guide finger. The target note just has to be on the same string.

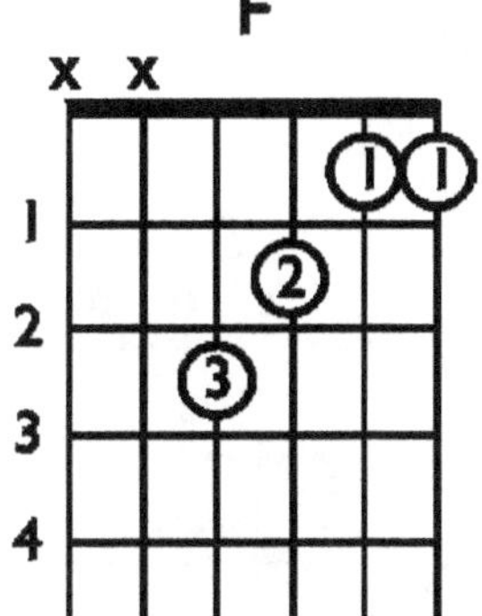

The F Chord is the 1st partial bar chord. Start from a C.

1. Hop the 2nd & 3rd fingers to the middle two strings.
2. Flop the 1st finger to press down two strings at once at 1st fret. The third finger bass note is more important than a clear first string.

Fingers should fall over on purpose, never by accident.

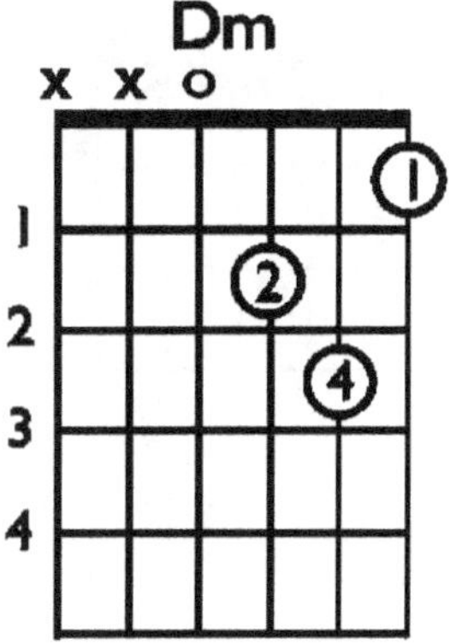

Dm or the D minor chord, is the relative minor of F major. Using the 4th finger for the 2nd string is essential to alternate bass notes. Remember that the 2nd finger is a shared finger between F and Dm and should not be lifted.

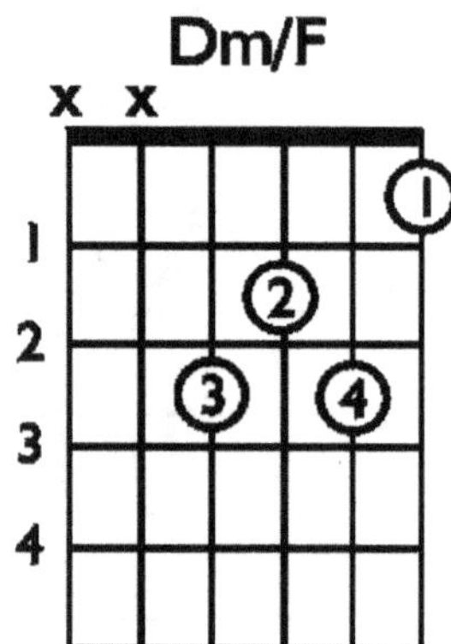

The slash chord is a new kind of chord symbol with an exception to the bass note rule.

The bass note rule makes the lowest D note the bass note of the Dm chord.

Place a backslash and the F note name after the chord symbol, the bass note is changed to the F note while keeping the Dm chord or **Dm over F.**

Four Fretting Strategies

These strategies are listed from easiest to hardest.

1. **Shared finger** is the "if it ain't broke don't fix it" rule. Just don't move that finger!
2. **Guide finger** is like a shared finger, but it slides keeping contact with the string.
3. **Finger hopping** is like flying in formation. D to G and D to C also use this plan.
4. **Follow the leader** is the last fretting strategy. If there are no shared fingers, guide finger or finger hopping shapes, we are left with a leader finger. The bass note, if fingered, is the leader.

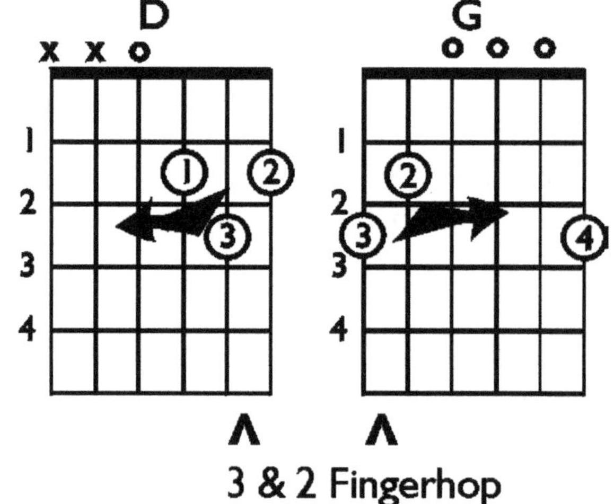

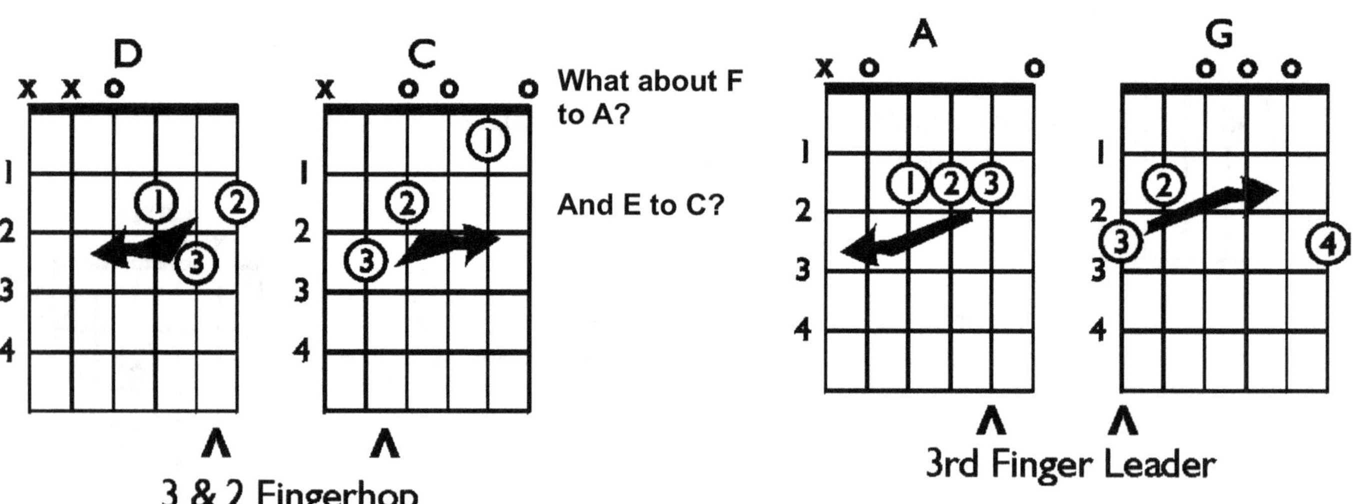

Fill in the names of the parts of the guitar

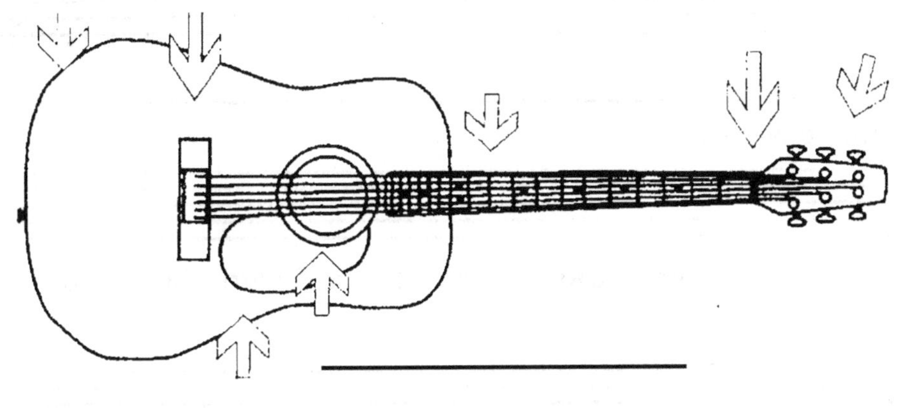

How are the fretting or left hand fingers numbered?

How are the picking or right hand fingers named?

Fill in these 8 bars with whole notes, half notes and quarter notes and rests.

Name the Treble Clef Staff Lines

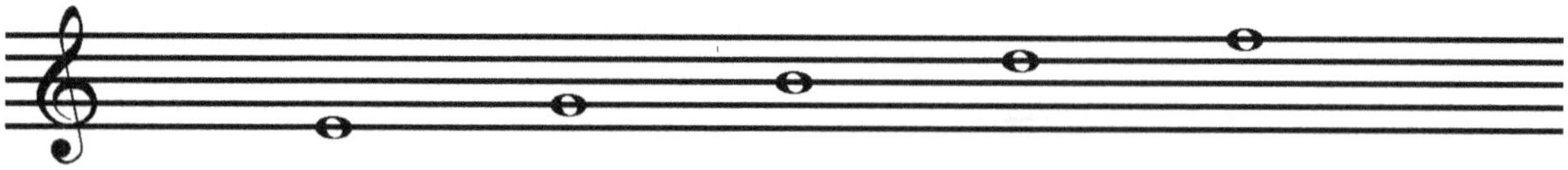

Name the Treble Clef Staff Spaces

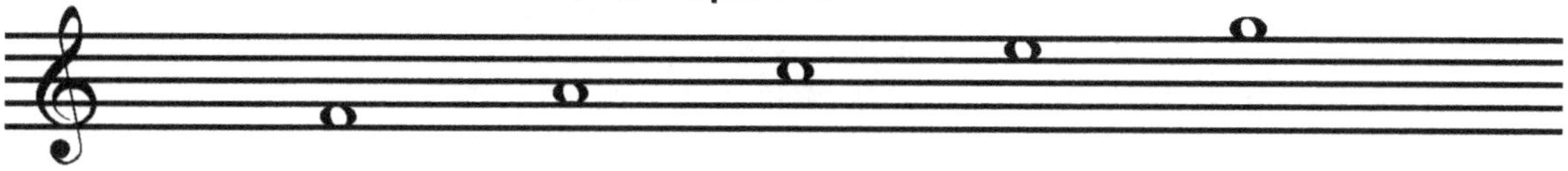

Name the Notes

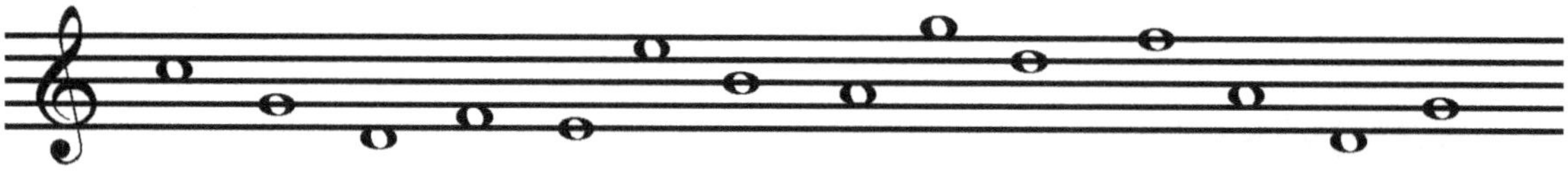

Draw these Notes

Alley Friday Guitar Cats Elvis Broke Down Fat Garbage Eat

Eat Cat Down Friday Alley Fat Garbage Elvis Guitar Broke

What are the names of the open strings of the guitar and how are they numbered?

Lines

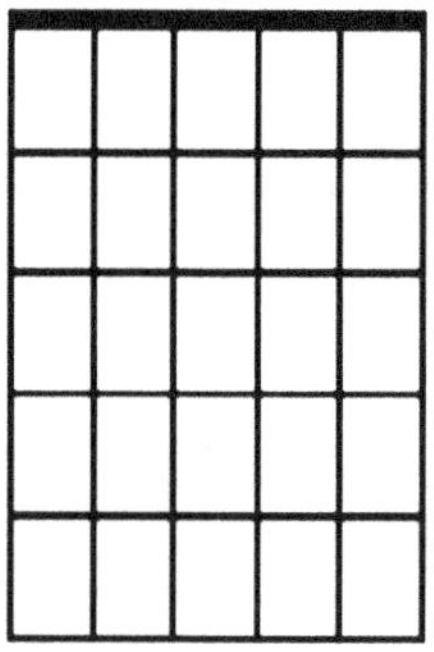

Spaces

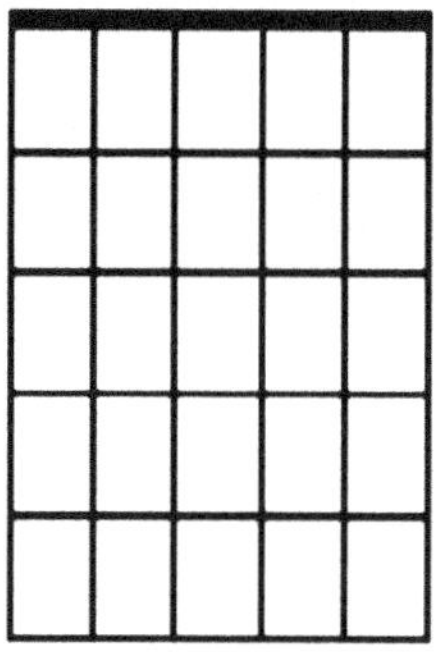

Natural Note Map

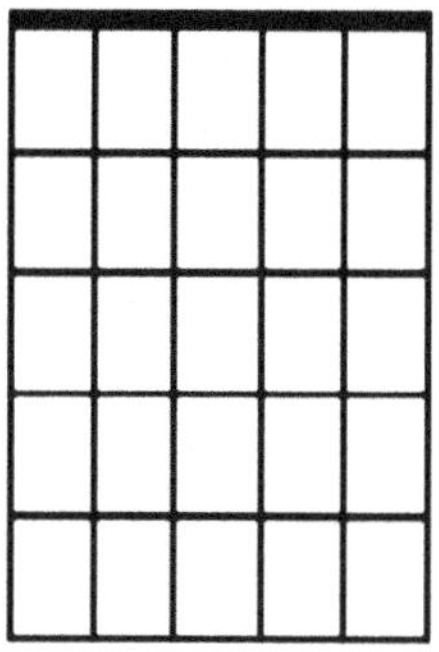

Draw pictures of the chords with note names using the note map.

Notate each of the chords. Look up the bass notes on the note map page.

Eighth Notes

Is it half as long or twice as fast? Both statements are true about eighth notes compared to quarter notes. In either case, we are dividing time by 2, cutting each beat into halves.

4/4 eighth note count: 1 and 2 and 3 and 4 and
3/4 eighth note count: 1 and 2 and 3 and

pick or strum down on the numbers and up on the and.

Mixed 1/4 & 1/8 Note Rhythms

These rhythms are mixes of quarter notes and eighth notes.

Play each of these exercises with your chord changes and with your notes as well.

Use some of the upcoming blank staves to experiment with 4/4 and 3/4 time signatures and these note values. Remember that the time signature sets the number of beats per measure. 3/4 has time for 3 quarter notes or 6 eighth notes and no more.

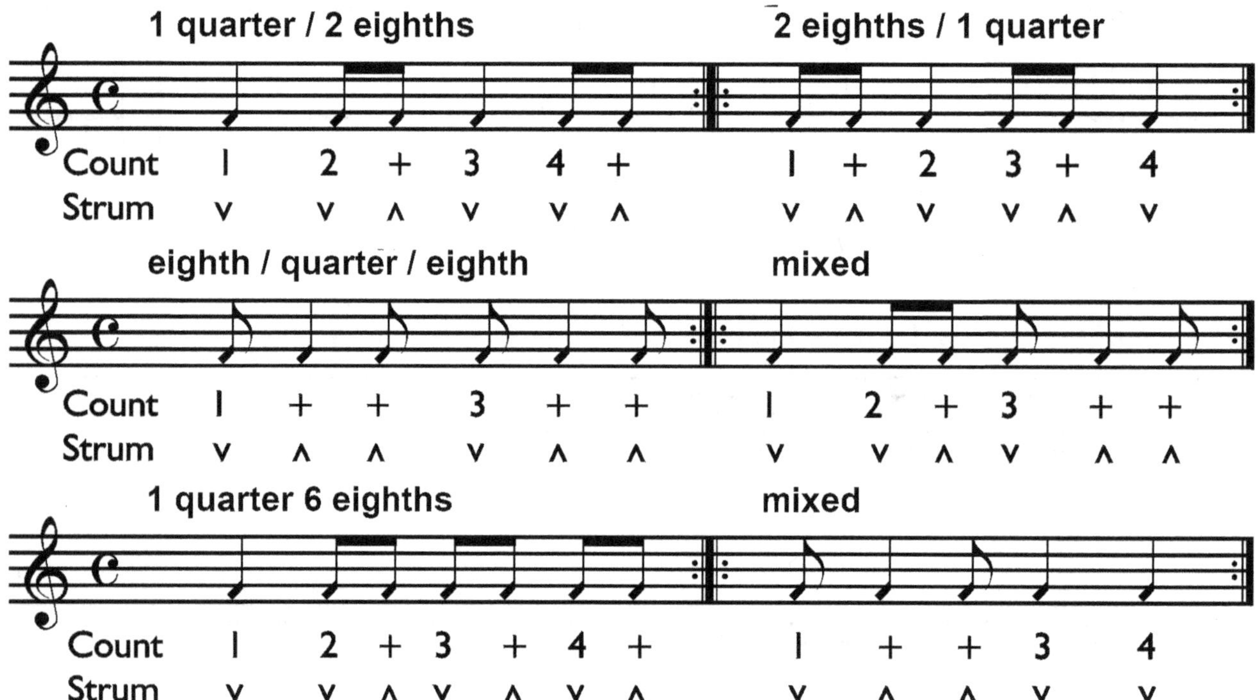

The rhythms we use are in everyday speech. Here are a few examples.

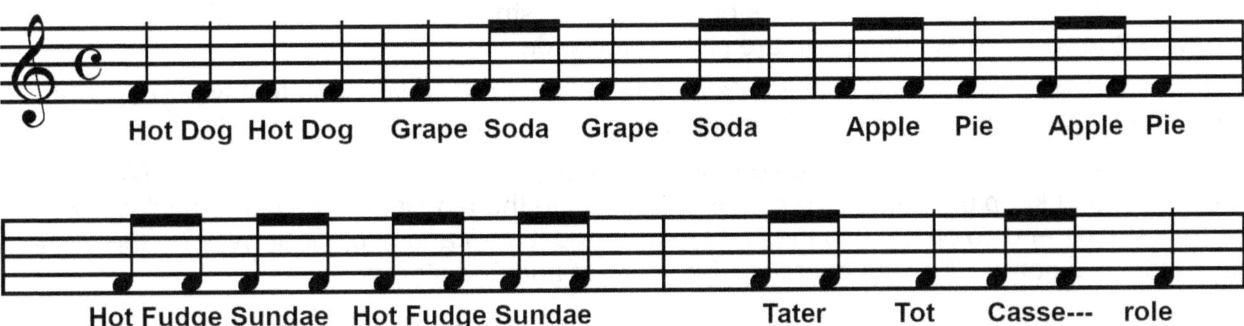

Draw exercises with two measures per line.

First, place a clef and a 4/4 time signature, then draw bar lines: middle first then the end of the staves. Add chord symbols at the correct place just after the correct bar lines.

Alternating Picking

Start with the 1st string, moving the pick only enough to strike the single string. If the pick moves more than twice the width of the string you are picking too wide.

Chant the exercise count slowly out loud a couple of times before you imitate it with your pick. Use all down strokes at first then switch to down/up strokes.

Remember: Down on the numbers up on the ands. Keep saying the count as you go. Move to the next lower string and keep the count. Work your way down to the 6th string then come back up to 5th and then 4th strings and so on back to the first string. Keep it slow and keep your eyes on the picking hand. Here are some 1/8 notes exercises for your 1st and 2nd strings.

Dots & Ties

Ties are rhythmic glue. Tying a half note to a quarter note makes a three beat note. Dotting a half note also makes it three beats long. Dots add 1/2 value.

Tying a quarter note to an eighth note makes it worth one and a half beats. Dotting the quarter note also makes it worth one and a half beats.

Dots work only within the measure. Ties can cross the bar lines. The number of beats tied is calculated by basic addition.

Basic rock 1 is straight eighths with an accent on two and four.

Basic rock 2 accents the "and" of two tied through beat three after which the "and" of three leads to four and.

This beat feels like bouncing off of two and bouncing into four.

Strum down on the numbers and up on the ands.

Strum: down down up up down up

Count: 1 2 and, and 4 and.

Basic Rock 1 **Basic Rock 2**

1 + 2 + 3 + 4 + | 1 2 + (3) + 4 +

Cut Time

Cut Time is the half time feel. Quarter notes get counted like eighth notes.

Count off sets the tempo and gets everyone to start together. We usually count off twice or more before the actual downbeat.

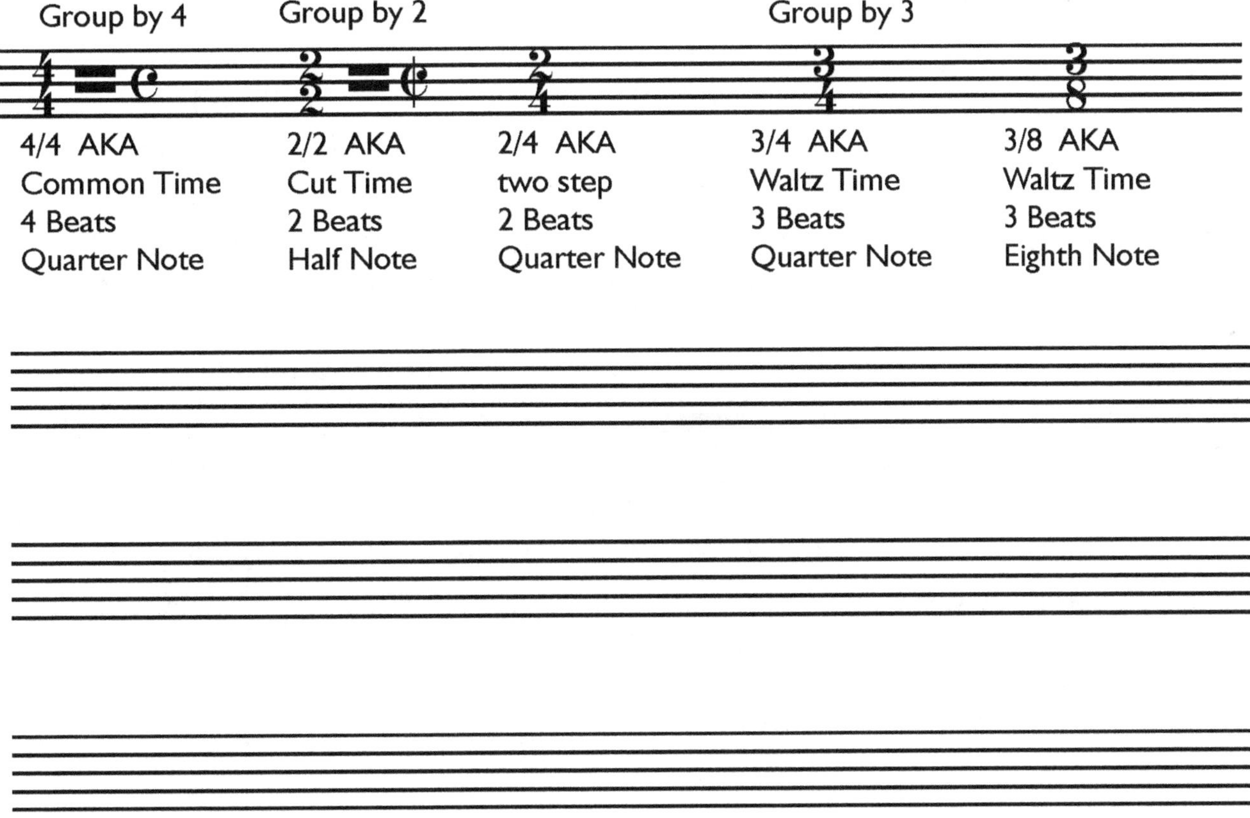

Triplets and Compound Meter

Three is another division of rhythm in music. In 4/4 time, triplets are indicated by the "3" over or under the group of three notes. This is called a triplet sign and squeezes three notes into the time normally reserved for two (eighth notes). **Straight eighth notes walk step by step. Swing eights skip along.**

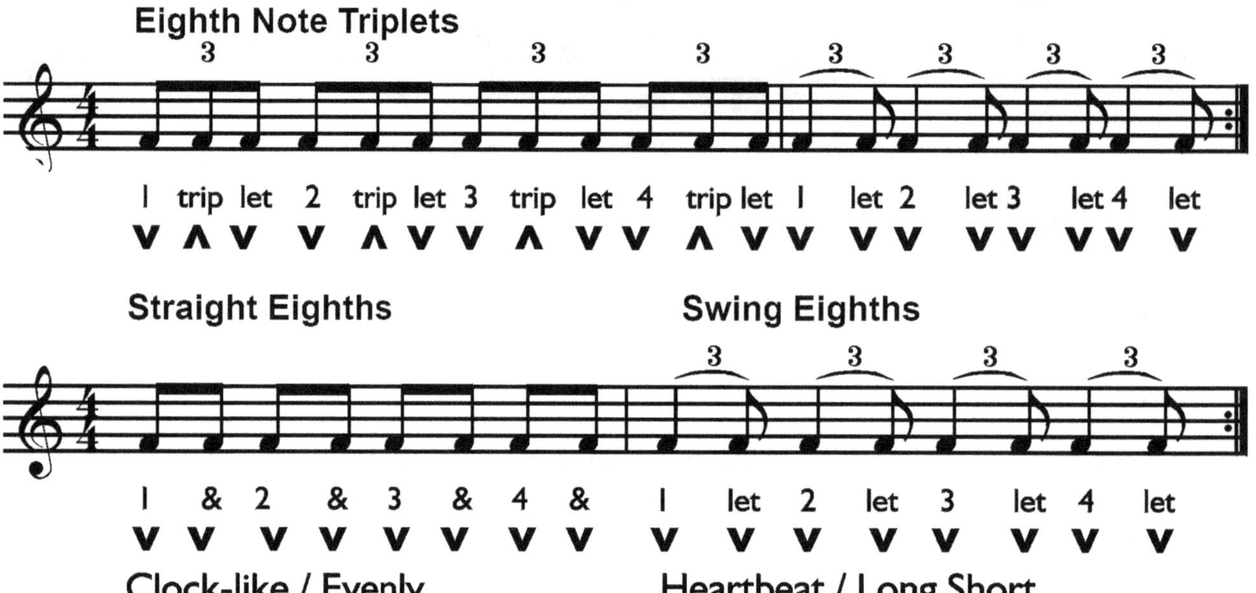

Triplets can be fixed as the normal division of rhythm with compound meters such as 6/8 & 12/8. These time signatures usually have a main pulse at beat 1 & 4 (in 6/8) and 7 & 10 (in 12/8).

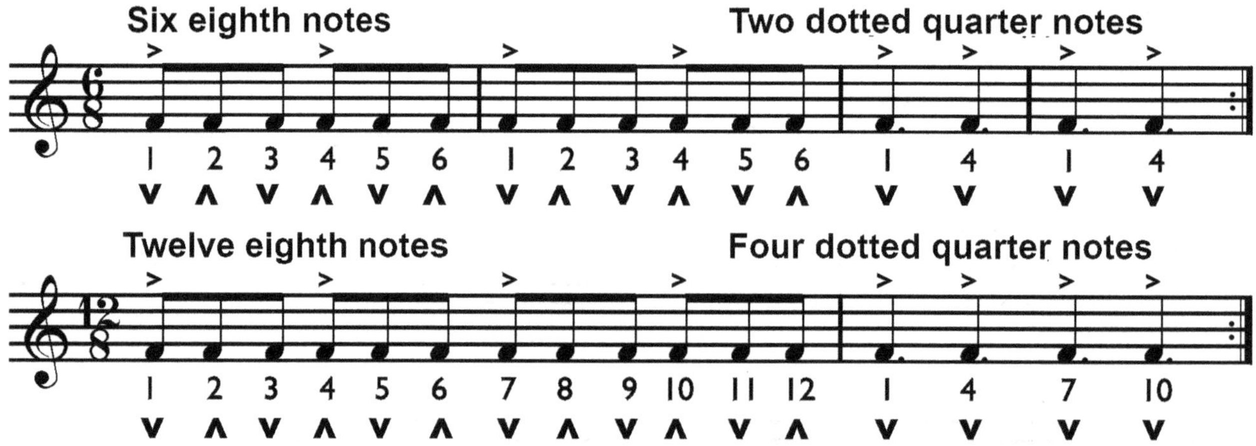

The Shuffle and Swing

Swing Indicators

A triplet without the trip is the best way of describing basic swing. This fascinating rhythm is the heartbeat of American Music.

Straight eighths are even and clock like tic tock tic tock

(1 + 2 + 3 + 4 +).

Swing eighths are a heartbeat lub Dub lub Dub

(1 -let2 -let3 -let4 -let).

Swing feels can be indicated at the beginning of the tune with the swing indicator telling us to play all eighths as swing eights or all dotted eighth sixteenths as swing eights.

More Mystery Tunes

Rests and Fretting Hand Muting

The Chicken Principle

The lethal and stupid game of chicken can be an analogy for how to move the fretting hand. The car and pedestrian version works best. The pick is the car. The fingers are the pedestrians. Jump out of the way at very last moment. Jump in at the very last moment.

This creates a **legato** or long sound. Each note rings for its entire time value. The opposite of this sound is called **staccato** or short. Each note is immediately muted after being struck.

Make the movements of both hands as simultaneous as possible. Play slowly and keep the notes ringing as long as possible then cut them off at the right moment. **Rests are moments of silence.**

Rests can be created by either hand but picking hand muting, palm muting, is usually more of a special effect.

Pinky, Fall Over and Don't Squeeze Muting

For chords such as **D**, **E**, **A** or any chord with lower open strings, extend the 4th finger across the fingerboard and touch the strings to stop the vibrations: the **pinky mute**.

For chords such as **G**, **C** or any chord with open interior strings, release the pressure on the strings without lifting and let the fingers fall over onto the strings for the **fall over mute!**

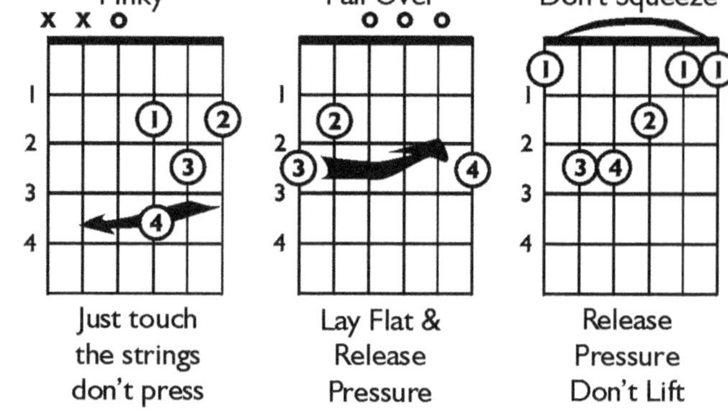

For bar chords and single notes, leave the finger(s) in place and release the pressure but don't lift to create silence: the **don't squeeze mute.**
Play a whole note long chord then stop it with a whole rest. Repeat until smooth.

Next we play a two beat long half note chord and rest for two beats, counting all the time as we do this.

Then quarter note chords with rests on each of the beats in turn then combinations of two notes on and two notes off. Think of a rest as if you are turning the note off like with a light switch instantly.

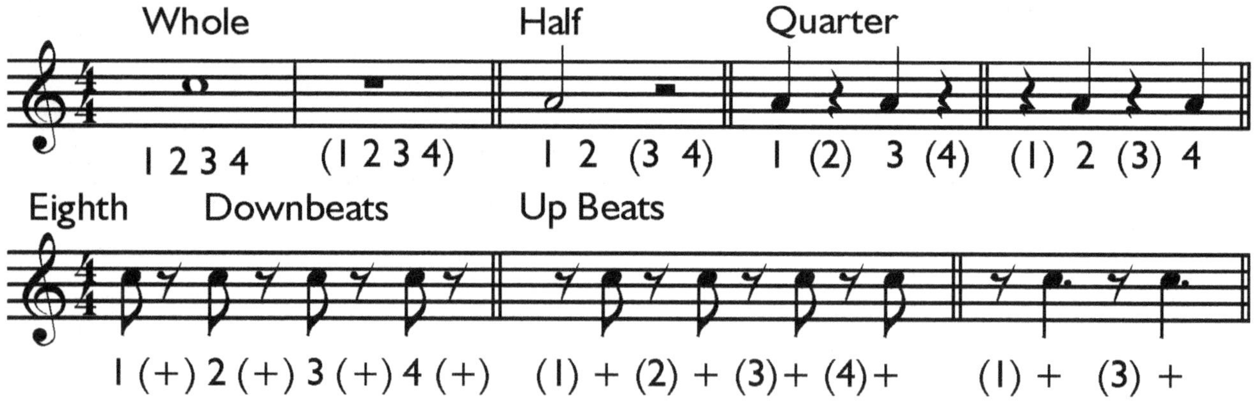

The back beat chank and chick are two of the most common usages of these muting techniques. While the kick drum is on beat 1 the snare drum will hit hard on beats 2 and 4, the back beats. The guitar plays bass note with the kick and the chord with the snare. The "chank" sounds like a chank.

Pick the bass note on beat one and three then strum beat two and four, muting the chord immediately after the strum, creating a staccato chord. The "chick" sounds like almost like a slap.

Pick the bass notes as before but mute the chord as it is struck making a percussive sound.

Notes on the 5th & 6th Strings

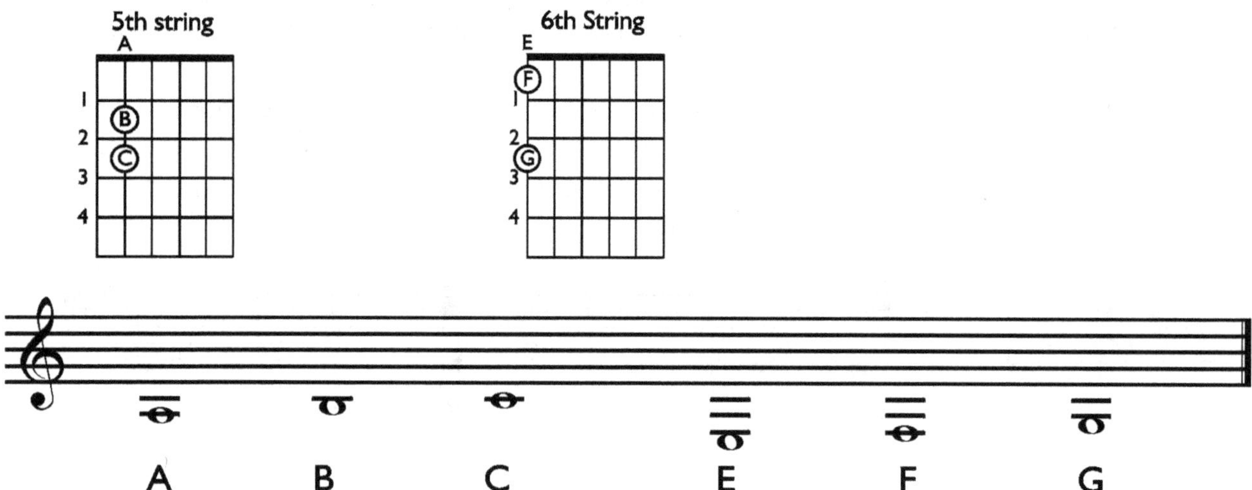

These are the very lowest notes on the guitar, the bass notes.

The 5th string has the open natural notes: A, B at the 2nd fret and C at the 3rd. The 6th string has open natural notes: E, F at the 1st fret and G at the 3rd fret.

Count the Ledger Lines

Three lines down is F, hanging from it is E.

Two lines down is A, hanging from it is G.

One line down is C, hanging from it is B.

Counting lines is the quickest way to read ledger lines.

Bass notes on beat one

Bass Note Rule: the primary bass note of any chord is the lowest note that has the same note name as the chord. For example: C for the C chord and G for the G7. Place the 3rd finger at third fret for these bass notes before placing the other fingers. Use the note map to find locations.

Bass notes get highest priority because they happen on beat one.

The bass notes of A and E chords are the open 5th & 6th strings. The bass note A belongs to all "A" something chords: Am, A7 and more but not Ab or A#. These are different notes one fret lower or higher than A natural.

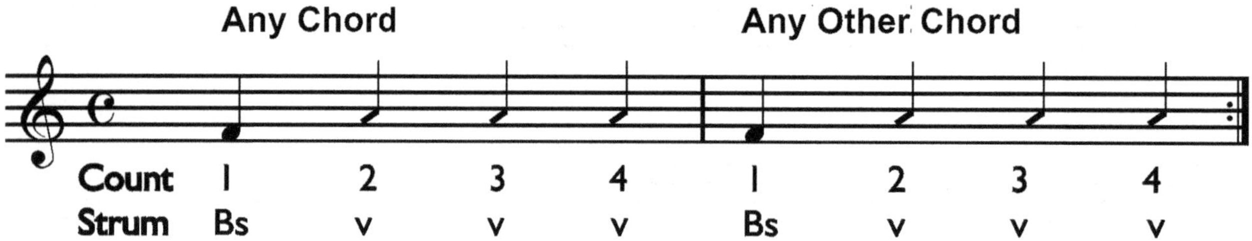

Bass Notes & Chord Strums

Bass notes are most often played on beat one with the thumb (pulgar) with strums following on the remaining beats. Pick the bass note only on beat 1. Pluck or strum the higher strings for beats 2, 3, and 4.

Play these exercises using bass notes. Look them up on the note map.

Flat & Sharp Bass Notes

The 5th String Bb/A# is at 1st Fret and C#/Db is at 4th Fret. The 6th string has F#/Gb at 2nd fret and the G#/Ab at the 4th fret. All bass notes are very important to memorize because of their importance in using moveable power chords and full bar chords.

Remember that bass notes get highest priority because they happen on beat one.

The bass notes of A, D and E are the open 5th, 4th & 6th strings. The bass note A belongs to the Am and A7 chords as well as any other A chord (not Ab or A#).

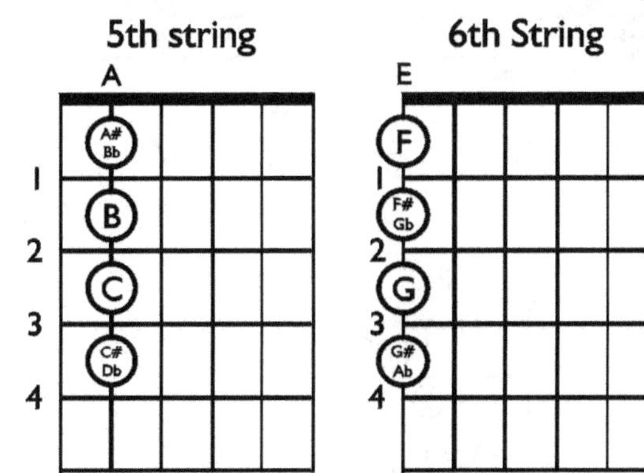

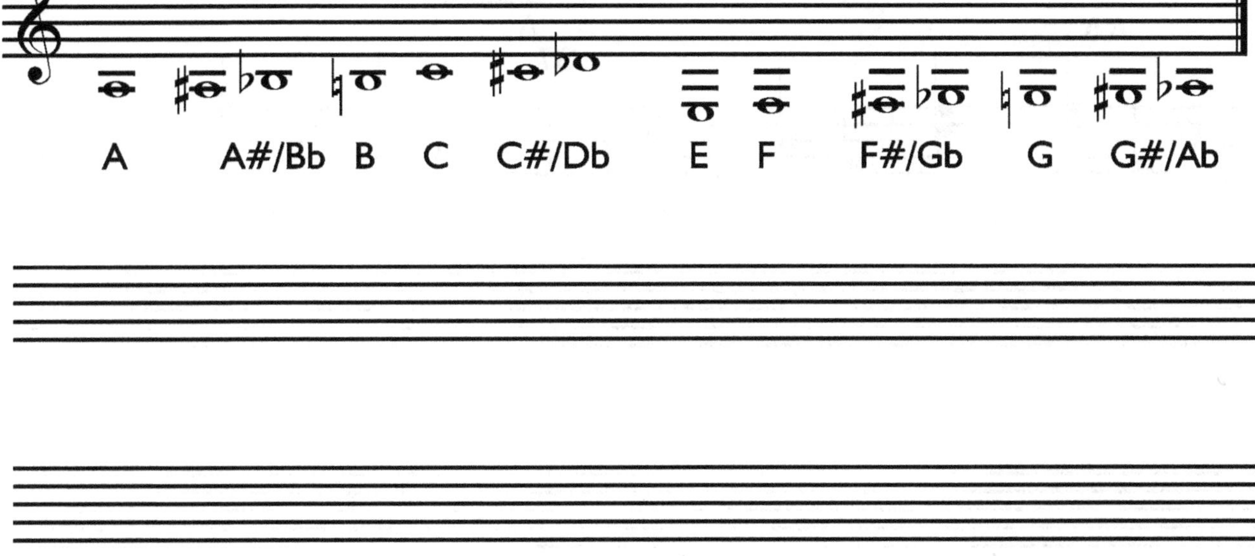

The Most Popular Bass Line in the World!

Music is full of bass lines moving from root note to fifth: alternating bass.

The root is the primary bass note. The fifth is the secondary bass note.

The momentary chord is called C/G. Pick the primary bass note and strum the upper part of the chord then pick the secondary bass note and strum the upper part of the chord again.

This is a good time to emphasize the time signature of cut time: a C with a line slicing through it vertically. This indicates a 2/2 count instead of a 4/4 count. A half time count means quarter notes get counted like eighth notes.

C to F Bass
D
1
2
3
4
E
C
F
G to C Bass
A
1
2
3
4
B
G
C
C
F
C
G7
C
F
C
G7
C

C
F
C
G7
C
G7
C
F
C
G7

More Mystery Tunes

Transposing Octaves

Take the previous tunes and transpose them up an octave and play them.

An 8va symbol can be placed over a section of notation ordering you to play everything one octave higher. Get used to it. You will need to sight read it.

Draw your notes and chords

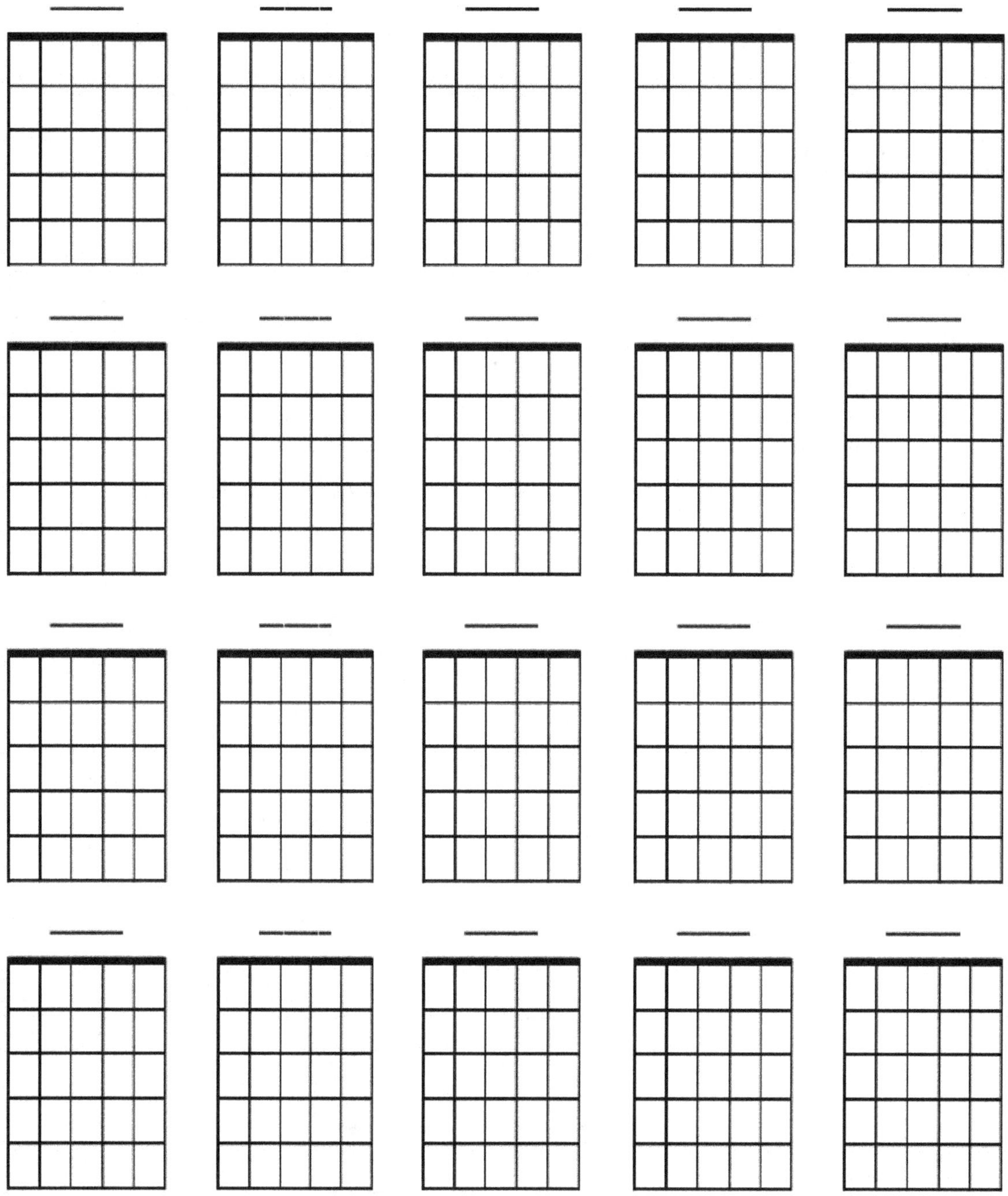

Identify the note and put it on the staff.

Write in the rhythm count below the notes.

Identify the note on the staff and plot its location on the map.

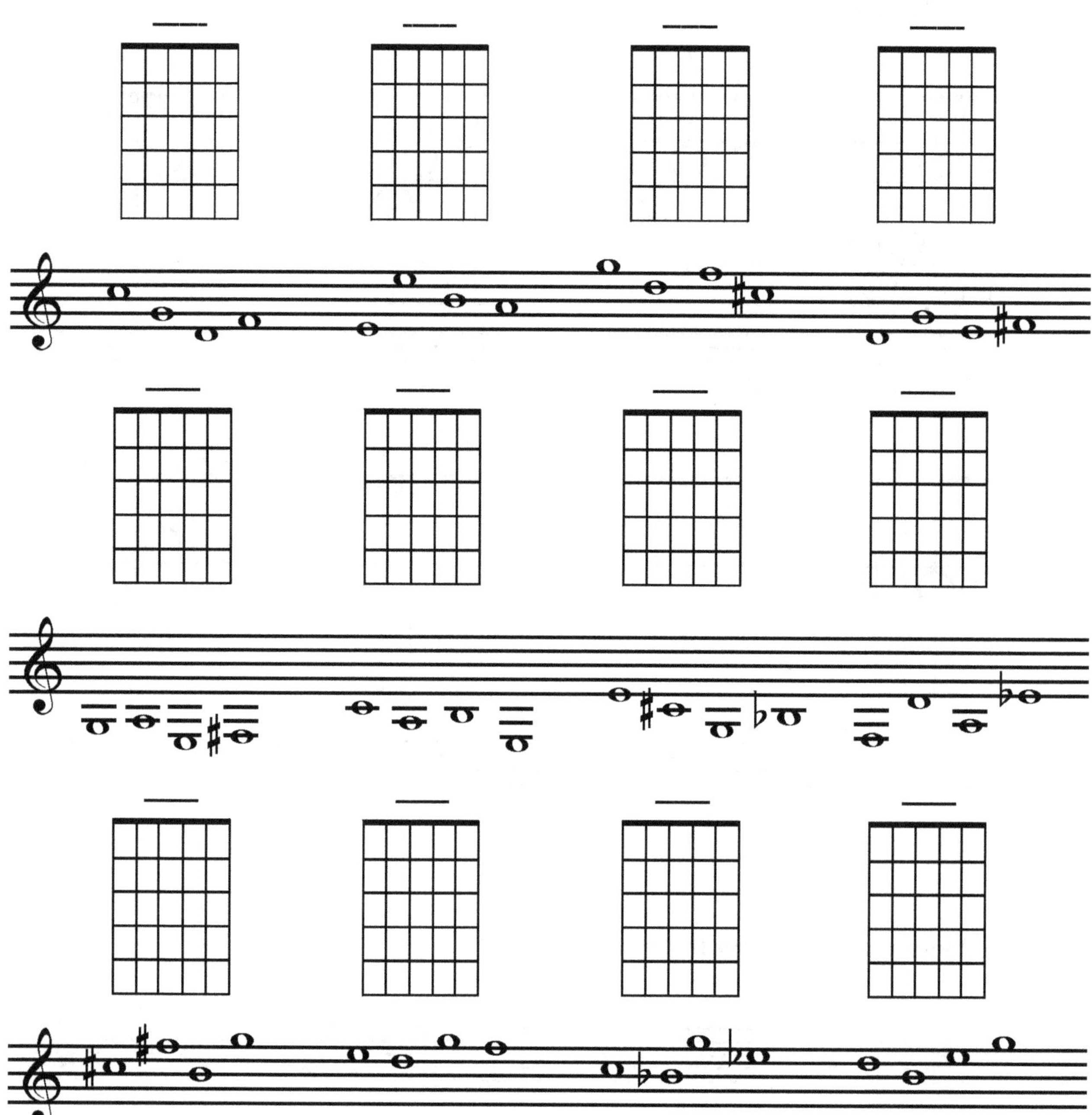

Cheap Tricks and Intervals

Cheap tricks are simple moves on the guitar which make great sounds. They also show us how chord names work. Just remember to count from the root note as one, not zero.

1. Lift the 2nd finger from the 1st string and expose the open E string. E is the 2nd note in the key of D major and the chord becomes Dsus2 (suspended second).
2. Placing the 3rd finger on the 1st string 3rd fret suspends the perfect 4th G and creates the Dsus4 (suspended fourth) chord.

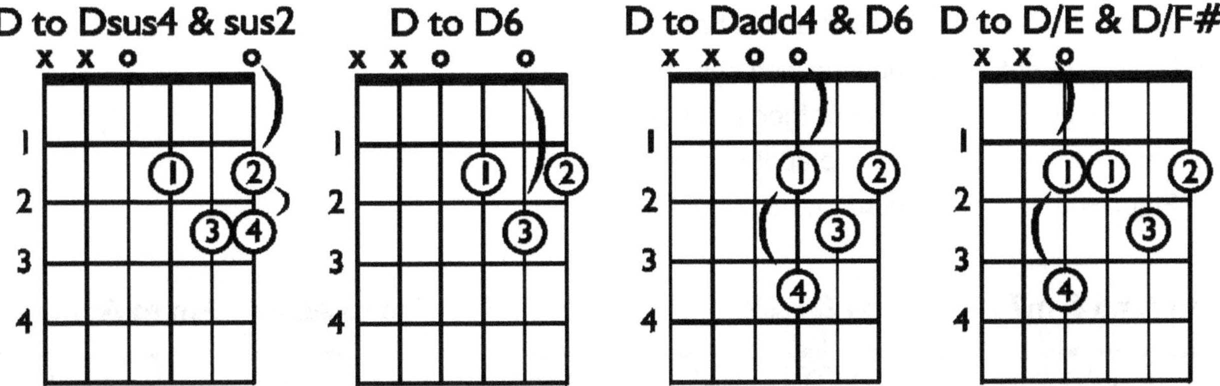

3. Lifting the 3rd finger exposes the major 6th and creates the D6 chord.
4. Lifting the 1st finger makes Dadd4. The third, F#, is still in the chord so the fourth is added not suspended.
5. Adding the 4th finger on the 3rd string B is another D6.
6. Moving the 1st finger to the 2nd fret 4th string adds an E bass note for a D/E chord.
7. Add the F# bass note for a D/F# chord.

Tricks for A Major

1. Place the 4th finger on the 2nd fret 1st string for F# and play the A6 chord then, move it to the 3rd fret for the 7th note G and play the A7 chord.
2. Lift the 3rd finger from the 2nd string opening the B note, the major 2nd, to make Asus2 then place the 4th finger on the 3rd fret 2nd string for the perfect 4th D and the Asus4 chord.

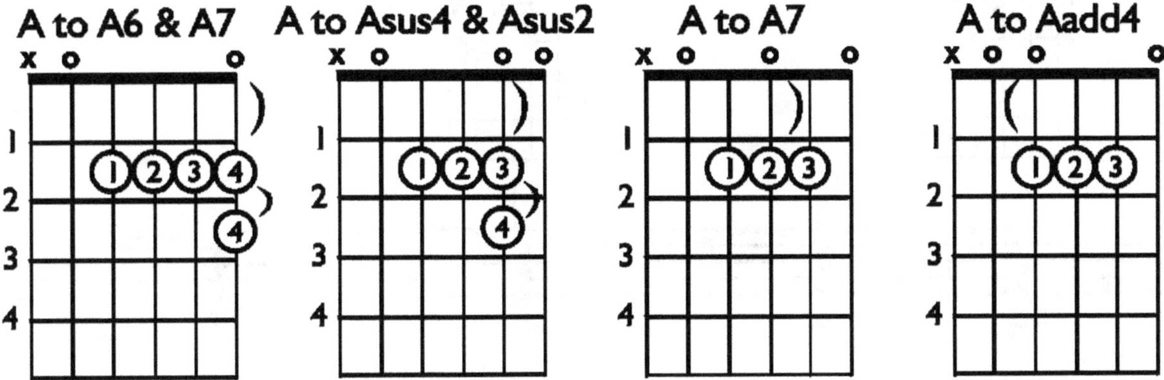

3. Open the 3rd string G for another voicing of the G7 chord.
4. Lift the 1st finger exposing the D and making the Aadd4 chord.

What About Am?

1. The 4th finger can grab the 6th F# and the 7th G creating the Am6 and the Am7 chords.
2. The note numbers remain the same as in A major with the same B and D notes being 2nd and 4th. The difference is that they resolve to the major 3rd C# in the key of A major and the minor 3rd C in the key of A minor.
3. The 3rd string open is the minor seventh creating a deeper sounding Am7 chord.
4. The fourth string lift adds the 4th.
5. The 5th string moves add B and C bass notes.

Cheap tricks is about experimenting with chord sounds.

1. Lift a finger or place a finger then listen to the sound.
2. Find out which note you are adding or exposing.
3. Figure out what the chord name should be.

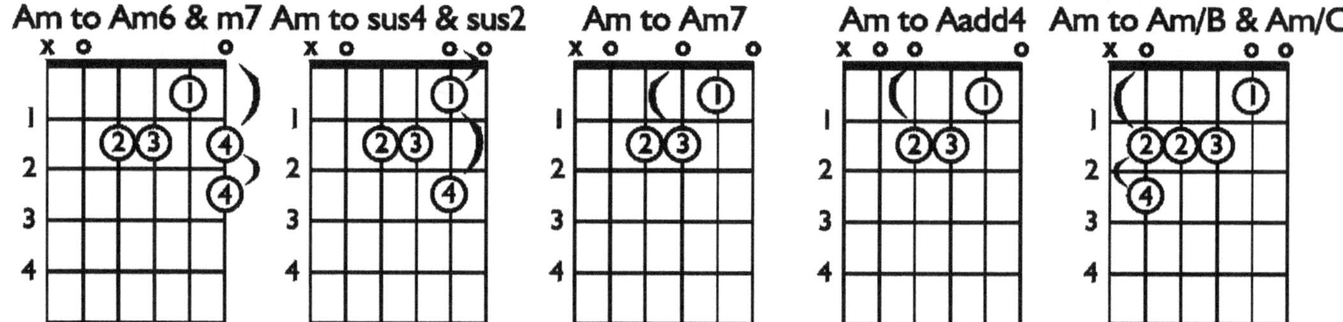

The Hammer On & the Pull Off is the the most important left hand technique for cheap tricks.

A **hammer on** is landing the finger very hard on the string behind the fret.

A **pull off** is plucking the string with a finger of the left hand.

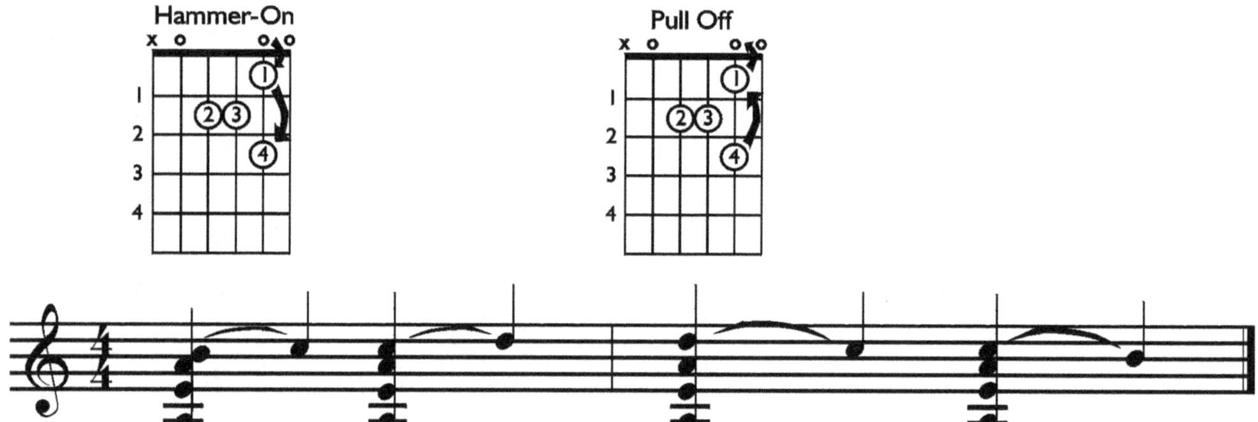

Three Chord Rock **One Four Five (I - IV – V) Tonic Subdominant Dominant**

The Mariachi chord order: Primera Segunda Tercera or 1st, 2nd and 3rd are correct in importance as tonic, dominant and subdominant ARE the order of importance of these chords. The numbered order is tonic, sub dominant and dominant, I, IV V, one four and five. I to V is much more common that I IV or any other combination.

Millions of tunes: classical, country, jazz, rock and blues use this three chord structure.

The **I - IV - V** is part of **both** the harmonized major scale and harmonized minor scale. All major and minor keys have the *same* harmonized chords.

Natural Half Steps **Triad Chords**

V V

I II III IV V VI VII I

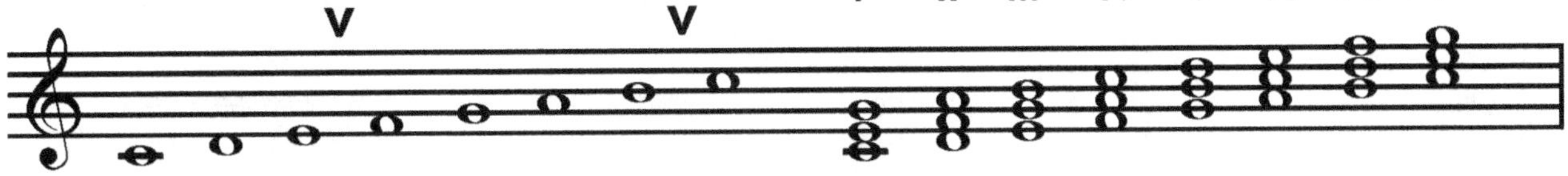

C D E F G A B C — C Dm Em F G Am Bdim C

1 2 3 4 5 6 7 8 — Λ Λ Λ

C F G

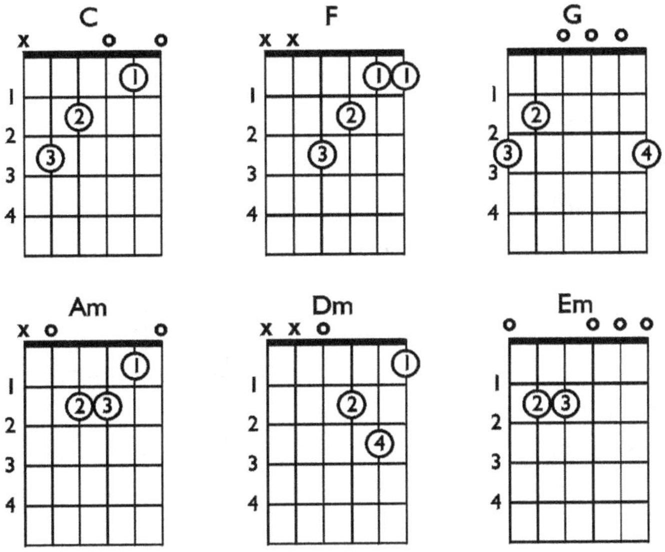

Am Dm Em

Let's play "You are My Sunshine" with the C, F & G. Start with the C chord, strum it over and over with a basic four/four beat. Try to find the first notes with your voice. The first note is always one of the notes in the background C chord. It is either the C, E or G note. Start singing the tune from each note. Only one note will work. At the word "happy" the chord changes and you need to figure out which of the other chords it went to. Is it F or G?

From that chord the next change presents the same kind of choice except between another pair or chords. From F chord the choices are C or G. From G chord the choices are F or C.

Other tunes are: "This Land is Your Land" and "Silent Night."

What is the number order of these chords? How about "All the Pretty Horses," "Sinner Man" or "Scarborough Fair" in minor?

If a minor chord doesn't work perfectly, but sounds better than either of the other two chords, try its relative major.

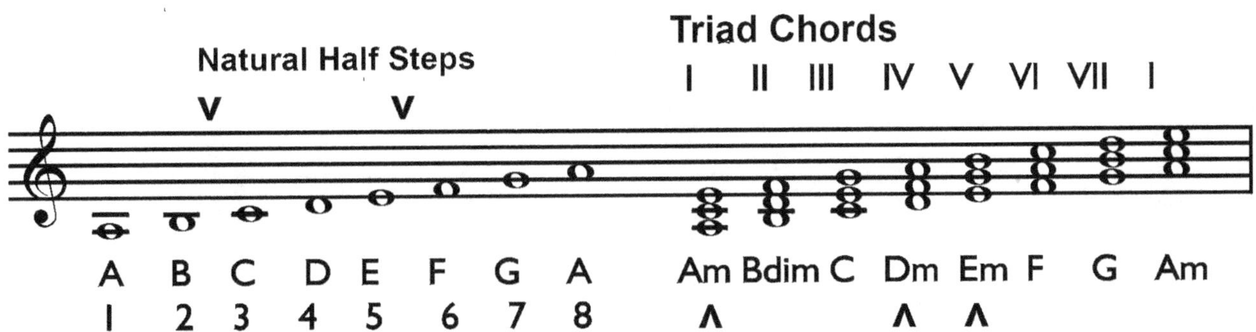

"Drunken Sailor" – Sea Shanty Traditional
"We Three Kings" - Christmas, Traditional
"Paint It Black" – Rolling Stones, Rock and Roll

Play Changes By Ear!

How about "Wild Thing" with A, D & E majors?

You can play it in the key of C but it will sound more like "La Bamba" which has the same chord progression.

Each basic guitar key is listed on this table in I IV V order along with the relative minor key.

Most modern music shifts between major and minor chords pretty freely and any chord in the key can become the central chord or the home chord of a song.

In other words a song might be in the key of C but you spend most of the time on a G7 chord.

I	(Im)	IV	(IVm)	V	(Vm)
C	(Am)	F	(Dm)	G	(Em)
G	(Em)	C	(Am)	D	(Bm)
D	(Bm)	G	(Em)	A	(F#m)
A	(F#m)	D	(Bm)	E	(C#m)
E	(C#m)	A	(F#m)	B	(G#m)

Why do we have different keys?

Have you ever tried to sing a song and it was either too high for your voice or too low? Didn't you wish you could fix that, maybe by making it a little lower or higher?

The basic reason for keys is that our voices have limited ranges. Try "She'll Be Comin' 'Round the Mountain" starting on a G Chord using the G, C and D then start on the A chord with A, D and E. That makes the song a little higher. To be much higher try the key of C.

V Can Be V7 / Dominant Seventh

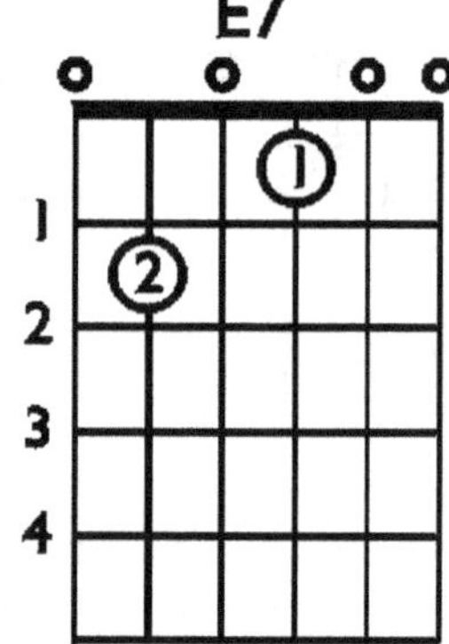

The number 7 is important. The note added to G chord to make a G7 is the note F. It has to be F something because F is the 7th note counted from G.

The major and minor chords so far have been triads or three note chords.

One kind of four note chords are called seventh chords. They are major 7th (maj7), minor 7th (m7), dominant 7th (7) and minor 7th flat 5 (m7b5).

Of these extended chords, only the dominant 7th gets used with triads often in traditional folk music. The only natural dominant 7 is the fifth chord of the major or minor harmony. Any dominant 7 chord is some key's V chord.

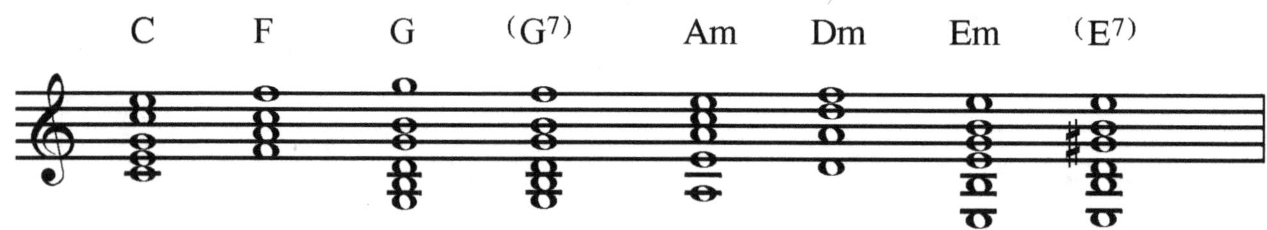

The Five of Five (V of V)

Secondary Dominant

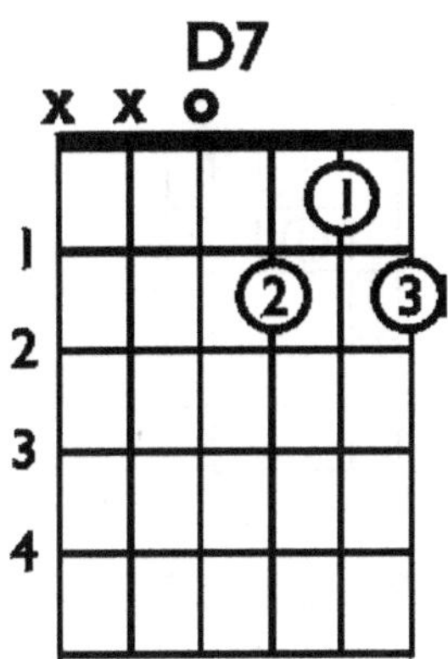

In the key of C, the 2nd chord (II) is a minor chord, Dm. If you see a D7 we are not in the key of C anymore. D7 is the V7 of the key of G; G7 is the V7 of C. D7 is the V of V also known as the secondary dominant.

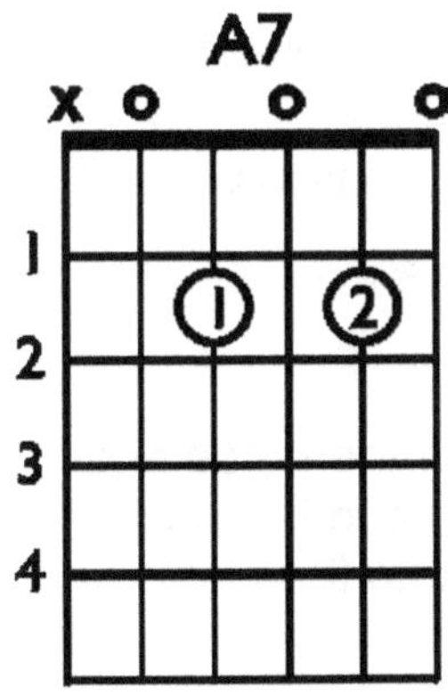

This a key center change to a neighboring key. If we are playing in the key of C, the key shifts to G at the moment the D7 is played, then returns to the key of C with the G7. This also helps determine which scale(s) the lead player uses for soloing and is one of the key tricks of the blues.

B7

G7 is the V7 of C and Cm
E7 is the V7 of A and Am
A7 is the V7 of D and Dm
D7 is the V7 of G and Gm
C7 is the V7 of F and Fm
B7 is the V7 of E and Em

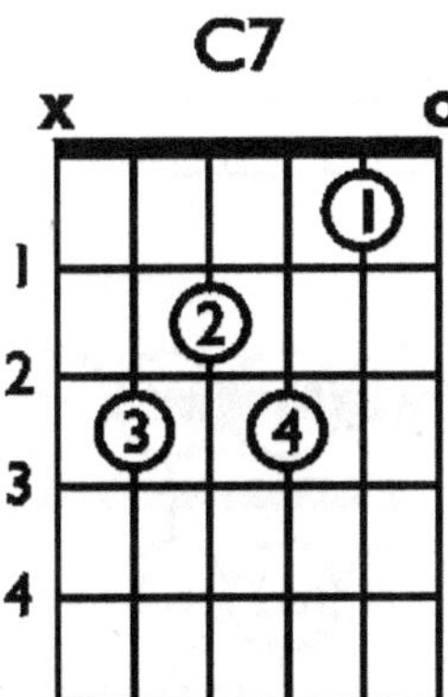

You can play a chain of secondary dominant chords. The V of V of V etc. The old timers called this **going around the horn**.

More Dominant 7 Voicings

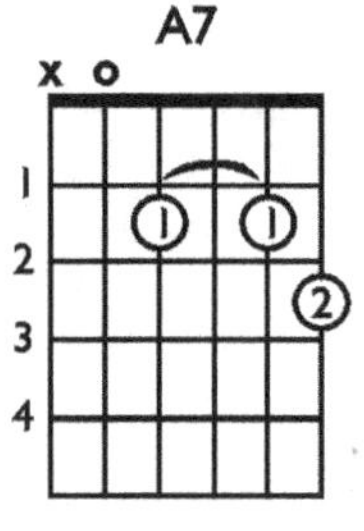

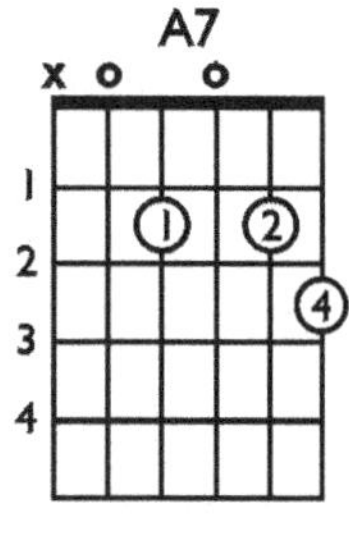

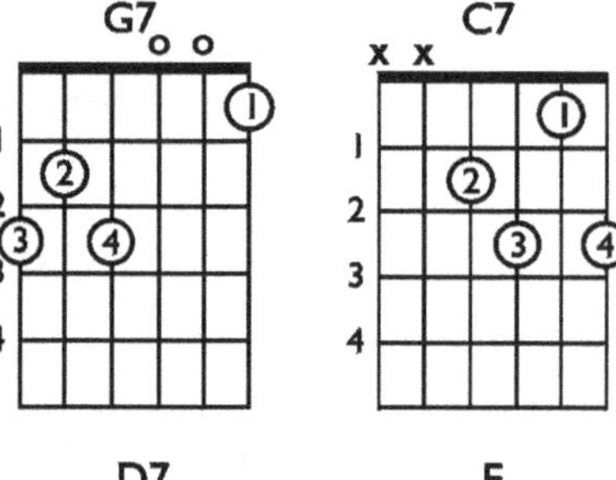

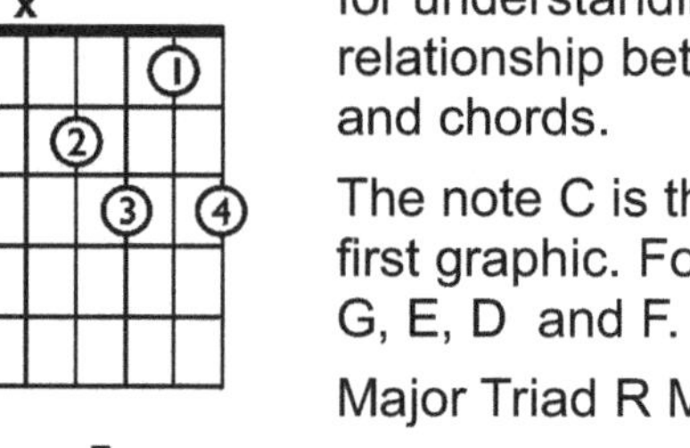

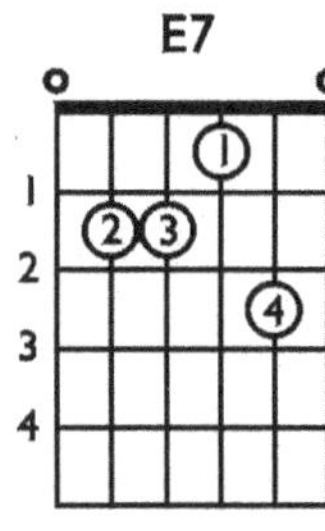

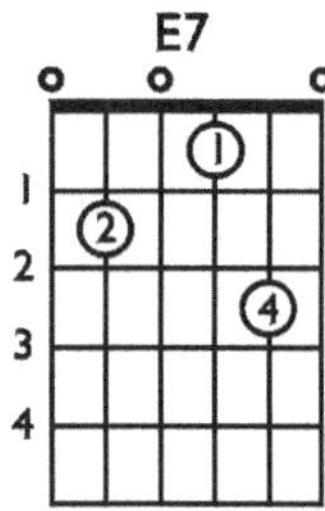

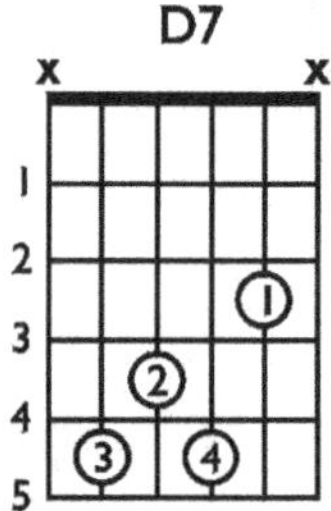

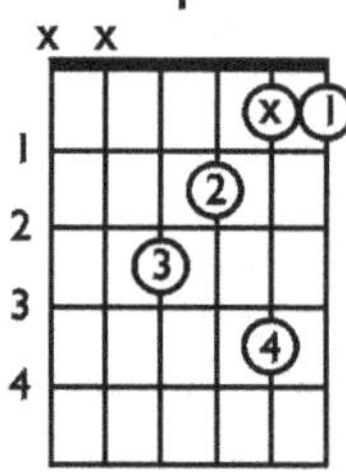

Interval Maps

Interval maps are a great tool for understanding the relationship between notes and chords.

The note C is the root in the first graphic. Followed by A, G, E, D and F.

Major Triad R M3 P5

Minor Triad R m3 P5

Dom. Seventh R M3 P5 m7

Identify all of the notes and chords you have learned as intervals within the chord or melody.

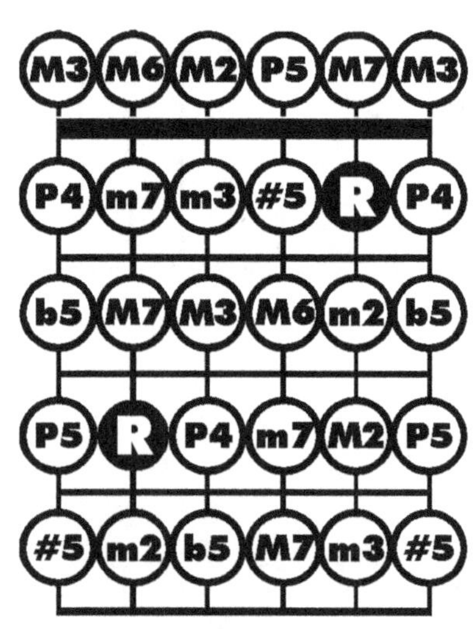

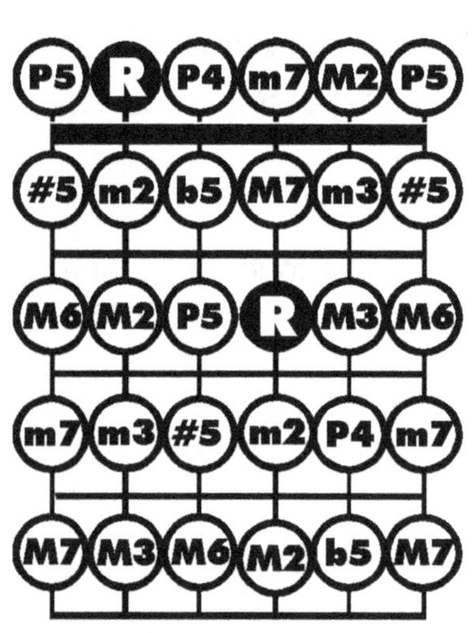

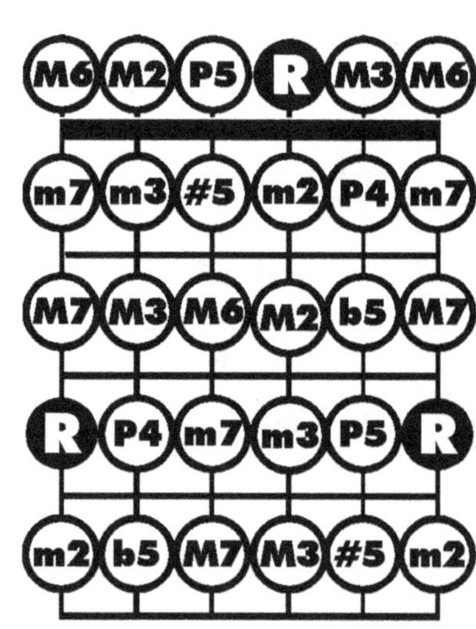

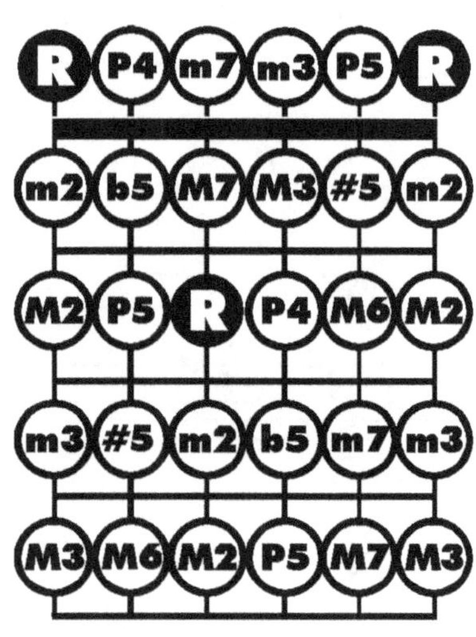

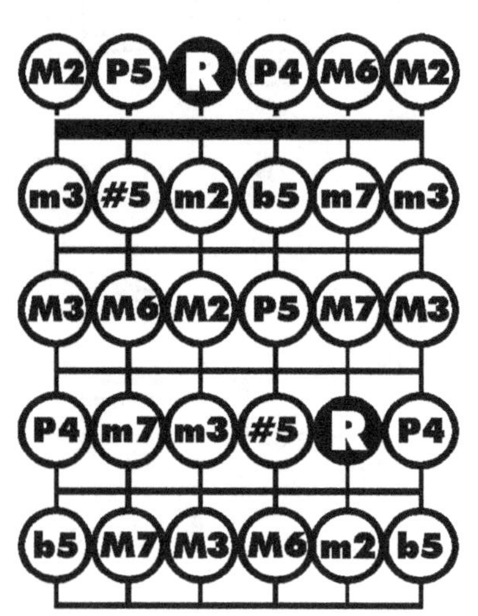

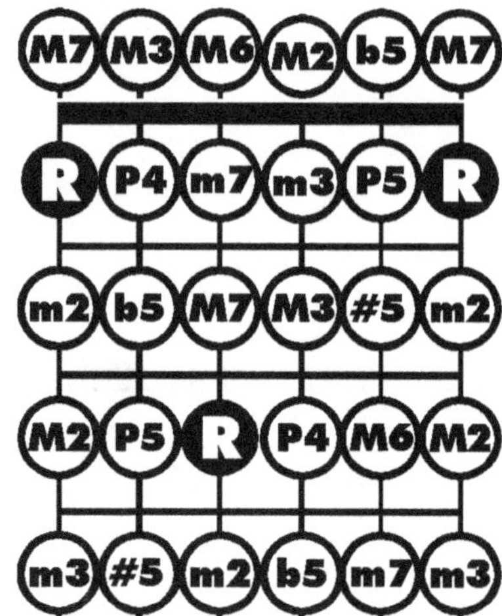

The Four of Four

The opposite of the five of five is also a key change only to the key of the IV chord instead of the key of the V chord. **In the key of C major this would be a Bb chord, the four chord of the key of F.** This is a relatively popular chord change in major keys and is usually called a flat seven chord in the key of C. Normally the VII chord of the key of C would be a Bm7b5 Chord or a G/B. If we flat the B we get a Bb major.

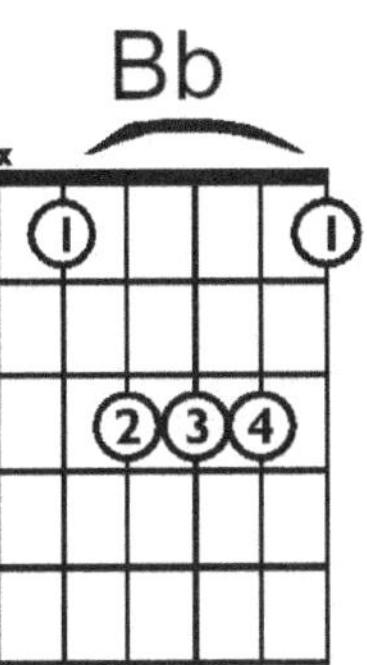

The "Hey Joe" chord changes start with the bluesy E7, as the V of the key of A major. It cycles from a C chord, the four of G, to the G which is the four of D to D which is four of the A major chord. C is the IV chord of G, G is the IV chord of D and D is the IV chord of A.

The four of four rarely happens in minor keys but is pretty common in major.

Four can change to Four Minor

Kind of a mirror of the V can be a V7 chord change, the IV chord can become a Four Minor chord. It is a change to the direct minor key of the root of the chord, from A as the IV chord of E to Am as the I chord of A minor. It is almost never the IV chord of E minor as the original key is E major.

This classic eight bar blues pattern in E starts on the I chord, changes to the E7, the V of A major. Then it moves to the A chord. At that point the A transforms into Am minor and the key shifts to Am for just a moment then goes back to E and the key of E.

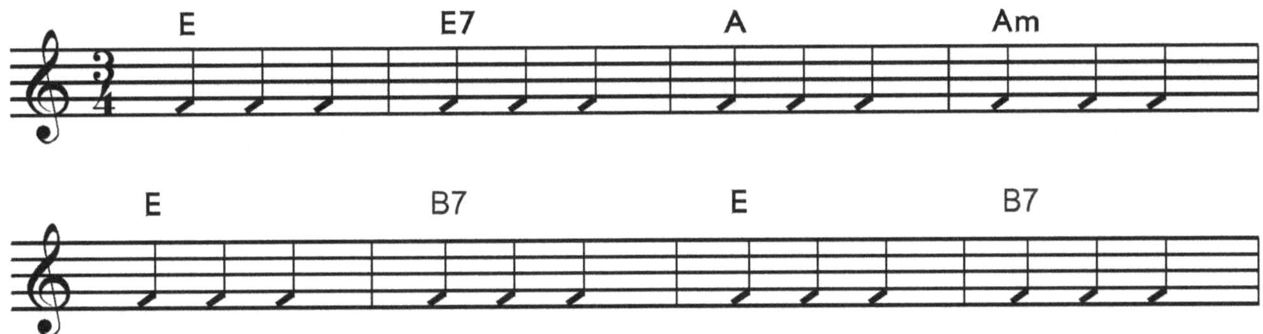

The Rule of Nine

If you are playing a dominant 7 chord you need to know what key you're in. You can count the scale **backwards five steps** to find the root of the I or Im chord. Or you can count **up four steps** to get the same note.

Up 4 or down 5, it adds up to nine Up 6 or down 3, up 7 down 2.

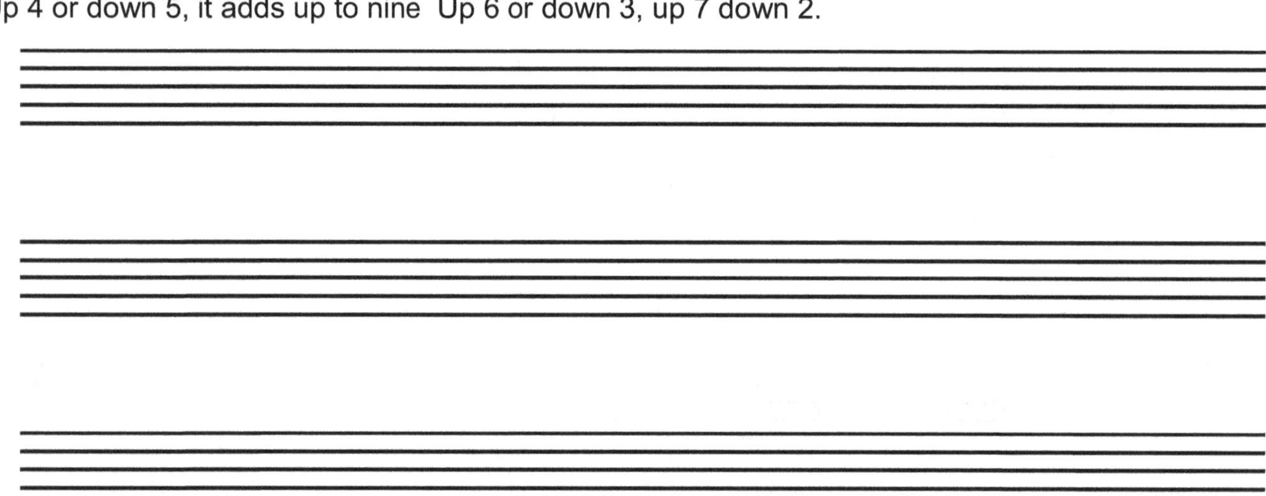

If you go to the V7 of any key, you can create a secondary dominant chord that leads to that key. Other chords from that key might show up now too, particularly the II chord.

Key of G/Em

These two tunes have a key signature: F # for the key of G/Em. Every F is sharped.

The next tune uses a half beat pick up note whose count is the "and of two" and leads into beat "one." The time is stolen from the last bar of the tune.

How would Mary Had a Little Lamb go in the key of G major? Or Yankee Doodle?

Changing the Key is the solution to the complaint "It's is too high!" or too low. Every note is moved the same distance in this case a 4th lower than C to G. Jingle Bells starts on the 3rd of the key of C so it must begin on the 3rd of the key of G: B.

Key of F/Dm

This tune has another new key signature: a Bb for the Key of F/Dm. It means that **Every B is Flatted.** There is also a note lower than D. What is that note? And where is it?

What? There was no B flat or B natural note in the song. Transpose the Ode to Joy to the key of F and the key of G.

Keys / The Circle of 5ths

Keys other than C/Am are made by flatting (b) or sharping (#) certain notes to maintain the major scale pattern. The do - re - mi scale interval structure has to be maintained to sound correct.

The two half steps are always between the 3rd and 4th notes and the 7th and 8th notes of the diatonic major scale. For diatonic minor they are between the 2nd and 3rd notes and the 5th and 6th notes.

Each sharp key add a sharp at the 7th step until all notes are sharp.
Flat keys add a flat at the 4th step until all notes are flat.

These keys can be indicated by a key signature written right after the clef in music notation. Each major key has a relative minor key.

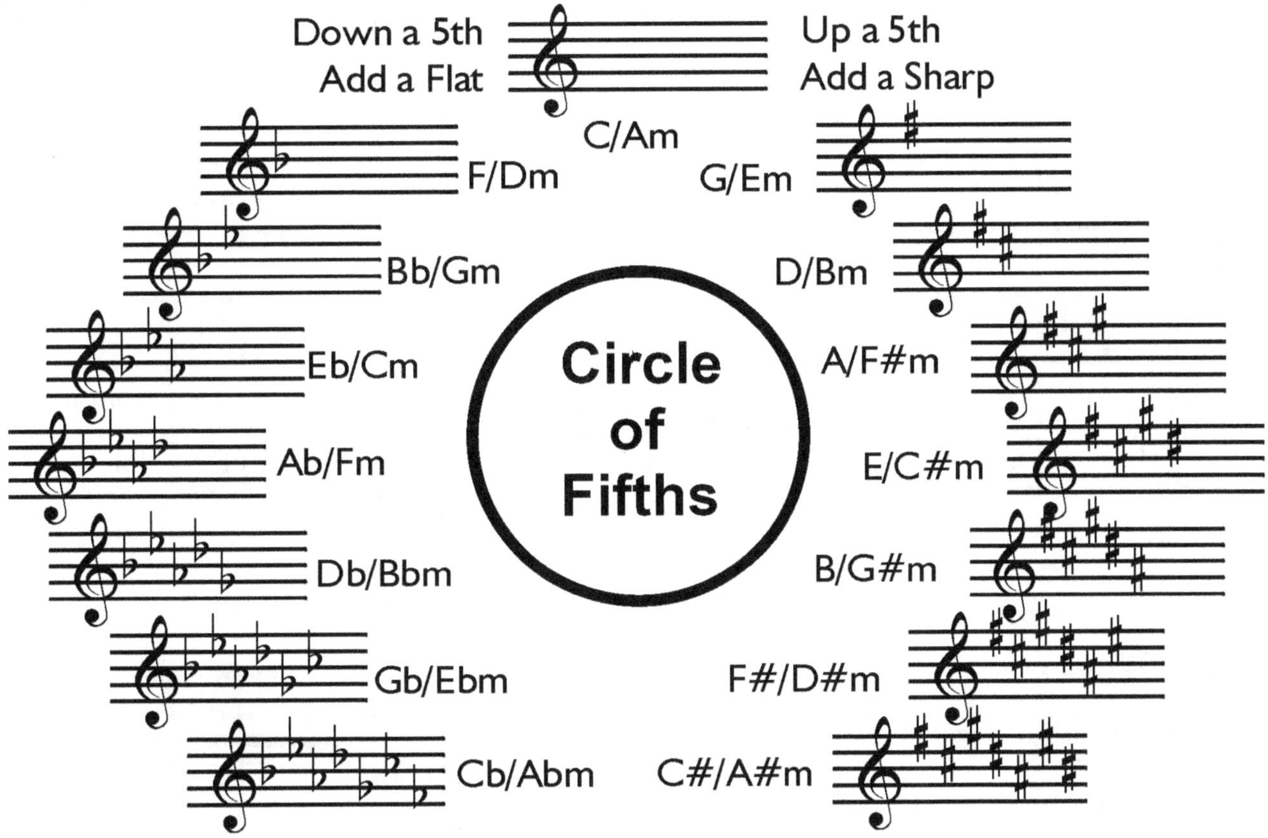

Each sharp key begins 5 major scale steps up from the root of the previous key and keeps its sharps.
Each flat key begins 5 major scale steps down from the root of the previous key and keeps its flats.

The keys of Db & C#, Gb & F# and Cb & B are enharmonic keys.

Nashville Numbering System

The major key & minor key spelling charts These are complete listings of all of the notes in all of the keys. Find the key you need along the top row and the scale step number along the side. it looks like the multiplication tables from elementary school for a reason. This information is just as unchangeable and fixed as the multiplication table.

These charts have been true for hundreds of years and are best memorized along with the key signatures, time signatures and much of the rest of the musical art. That way you never have to look it up again because you have it memorized.

Major Key Spellings

K	C♭	G♭	D♭	A♭	E♭	B♭	F	C	G	D	A	E	B	F♯	C♯	Chord
1	C♭	G♭	D♭	A♭	E♭	B♭	F	C	G	D	A	E	B	F♯	C♯	Maj
2	D♭	A♭	E♭	B♭	F	C	G	D	A	E	B	F♯	C♯	G♯	D♯	Minor
3	E♭	B♭	F	C	G	D	A	E	B	F♯	C♯	G♯	D♯	A♯	E♯	Minor
4	F♭	C♭	G♭	D♭	A♭	E♭	B♭	F	C	G	D	A	E	B	F♯	Maj
5	G♭	D♭	A♭	E♭	B♭	F	C	G	D	A	E	B	F♯	C♯	G♯	7
6	A♭	E♭	B♭	F	C	G	D	A	E	B	F♯	C♯	G♯	D♯	A♯	Minor
7	B♭	F	C	G	D	A	E	B	F♯	C♯	G♯	D♯	A♯	E♯	B♯	Half Dim

Minor Key Spellings

K	A♭	E♭	B♭	F	C	G	D	A	E	B	F♯	C♯	G♯	D♯	A♯	Chord
1	A♭	E♭	B♭	F	C	G	D	A	E	B	F♯	C♯	G♯	D♯	A♯	Minor
2	B♭	F	C	G	D	A	E	B	F♯	C♯	G♯	D♯	A♯	E♯	B♯	Half Dim
3	C♭	G♭	D♭	A♭	E♭	B♭	F	C	G	D	A	E	B	F♯	C♯	Maj
4	D♭	A♭	E♭	B♭	F	C	G	D	A	E	B	F♯	C♯	G♯	D♯	Minor
5	E♭	B♭	F	C	G	D	A	E	B	F♯	C♯	G♯	D♯	A♯	E♯	Minor
6	F♭	C♭	G♭	D♭	A♭	E♭	B♭	F	C	G	D	A	E	B	F♯	Maj
7	G♭	D♭	A♭	E♭	B♭	F	C	G	D	A	E	B	F♯	C♯	G♯	7

www.ingramcontent.com/pod-product-compliance
Lightning Source LLC
Chambersburg PA
CBHW081341090426
42737CB00017B/3247

* 9 7 8 0 6 9 2 1 9 3 5 2 5 *